SAMUEL SELVON was born in 1923 in Trinidad. His father was Indian and his mother Indian-Scottish. He attended Naparima College in San Fernando. During World War II he served in the Royal Navy Reserve. After the war he was a journalist in Trinidad until he emigrated to England in 1950. In England he worked as a civil servant while writing poetry and short stories, which were published in the *London Magazine*, the *New Statesman* and *The Nation*. His first novel, *A Brighter Sun*, was published in 1952. He went on to write *An Island is a World* (1954), *The Lonely Londoners* (1956), *Ways of Sunlight* (1957), *Turn Again Tiger* (1959), *I Hear Thunder* (1963), *The Housing Lark* (1965), *The Plains of Caroni* (1970), *Those who Eat the Cascadura* (1972), *Moses Ascending* (1975), *Moses Migrating* (1983), *Foreday Morning* (1989), *Eldorado West One* (1989). His work was also broadcast on BBC radio and television. Selvon took up various university appointments in the Caribbean, Great Britain and the United States. He received a number of awards including two Guggenheim Fellowships, in 1954 and 1968; Trinidad's Humming Bird Medal for Literature (1969) and honorary doctorates from the Universities of the West Indies and Warwick. He was married, with two sons and a daughter. In 1978 Selvon moved to Canada. He died in 1994.

MOSES
ASCENDING

Sam Selvon

Introduction by Mervyn Morris
University of the West Indies
Kingston, Jamaica

HEINEMANN

Heinemann Educational Publishers
Halley Court, Jordan Hill, Oxford OX2 8EJ
A Division of Reed Educational & Professional Publishing Limited

Heinemann: A Division of Reed Publishing (USA) Inc.
361 Hanover Street, Portsmouth, NH 03801-3912, USA

Heinemann Educational Books (Nigeria) Ltd
PMB 5205, Ibadan
Heinemann Educational Botswana (Publishers) (Pty) Ltd
PO Box 10103, Village Post Office, Gaborone, Botswana

OXFORD   BLANTYRE
MELBOURNE   AUCKLAND   GABORONE
CHICAGO
JOHANNESBURG   PORTSMOUTH (NA) USA

British Library Cataloguing in Publication Data

Selvon, Samuel
Moses ascending.—Caribbean writers series; 31
I. Title   II. Series
823'.912[F]   PR6052.E/

ISBN 0-435-98952-9

Printed and bound in Great Britain by
Cox & Wyman Ltd, Reading, Berkshire

98   99   00   01   10   9   8   7   6

*To my children
and the rest of the world*

Introduction

First published in 1975, *Moses Ascending* is, in a sense, a sequel to *The Lonely Londoners* (1956).[1] Characters from that earlier London novel are mentioned or actually reappear: Tolroy who sells a house to Moses; Big City, reportedly gone mad; Galahad, a substantial presence in this later book. Moses talks of a previous, unnamed work which sounds like *The Lonely Londoners*.

> There are those who will remember that if it wasn't for me, Galahad would of catch his royal arse in Brit'n. It was me who put him on his feet, share my basement room with him, console him in his distresses and lend him twelve and a half new pence when he was broke – in those days it was two-and-six, before they decimalize the currency. I have chronicled those colourful days in another tome...(44)[2]

'I', who? Moses, though an integrating consciousness, is neither narrator nor author of *The Lonely Londoners*. But at the end of that novel it is as though we have been reading the very book that Moses, cogitating, wonders if he could write: Moses and the omniscient author/narrator seem to merge. In *Moses Ascending*, which takes the form of first-person narration by Moses, much of the comedy requires that we glimpse, or think we hear, the author Selvon through the Moses mask.[3]

Near the end of *The Lonely Londoners* Moses is growing impatient of his role as unofficial welfare officer, as a sort of father confessor. The boys visit his room nearly every Sunday morning, 'like if they going to church', 'like if is confession'.[4] 'Lock up in that small room, with London and life on the outside, he used to lay there on the bed, thinking how to stop all of this crap, how to put a spoke in the wheel, to make things different'.[5] *Moses Ascending* gives us a Moses moving up and away from 'the boys', an older man, propertied, climbing above the struggle, anxious to be left in peace.

> The only thing I didn't want was to have any of the old brigade living in my house, and the rumour went around town that I was a different man, that I had forsaken my friends, and that there was no more pigfoot and peas and rice, nor even a cuppa, to be obtained, even if they came with gifts of myrrh and frankincense.(4)

The ironic religious imagery reminds us that the old Moses in *The Lonely Londoners* had indeed been something of a Christ–figure, absorbing the sufferings of the group. The new Moses, 'a different man' (the phrase recurs), has resentful 'thoughts about...how people want you to become involve, whether you want to or not.'(14) 'Third World', he says mournfully. 'It hard enough to live in one, and you-all making three.'(82)

In *Moses Ascending* Selvon topically updates his earlier accounts of immigrant life in London – *The Lonely Londoners*, some of the stories in *Ways of Sunlight* (1957), and another novel, *The Housing Lark* (1965). The plot of *Moses Ascending* involves the Black Power movement and illegal Asian immigration into Britain. It introduces the 'new generation of Black Britons'(15): Brenda speaks like the native she is: 'If I did shut my eyes', says Moses, 'I would of thought it was a nordic talking, the accent was so high.' (17) (With characteristic irony, that 'high' suggests not only superior status but also an odour of decay.)

Black Power, developing strength in Britain in the late 1960s and early 1970s, is ridiculed in *Moses Ascending*. Galahad is 'with it, man' (3). 'When Black Power come into vogue Galahad was one of the first to rally to the colours – I mean colour, of course. An American visitor from the Deep South indoctrinate him, and he became a rabid disciple...' (12)[6] In the account by Moses, contradictions are emphasized. BP, an American leader on a visit, begins a meeting with a call to prayer, 'but suddenly he was screaming out to kill all the whites and burn down the City of London, and as far as the pigs were concerned, hang one up in the doorway of every police station.' (93) Fighting oppression, BP drives a Mercedes and is deeply interested in the Party's funds. A Galahad date provokes the reflection by Moses: 'those who cry Black Power loudest usually have a white woman in tow, whether as lifeline or whipping-boy I leave to you.' (121) The Black Power proponents are presented as ready to exploit other people: they capture the basement of Moses' house; for the propaganda value to the Party, they allow Moses to languish in jail; they accept bail money from the white man, Bob, and are about to ignore the fact. It is surely prudent of Moses to fear that his precious Memoirs may be misconstrued by Black Power militants 'for their own purposes'. (139)

Resistant to Black Power, Moses nevertheless allows us several indications of the white racism to which Black Power is one response. The police, a negligible element in *The Lonely Londoners*, are a particular focus in *Moses Ascending*. They lock up Moses, a mere spectator. On a later occasion they arrest Galahad, Brenda and BP; asked for a reason, Bob, who is white, declares: 'Much against my will, I gravely suspect it is only because they are black.' (96) Whites are seen as of higher standing than blacks in Britain. Faizull notes: 'It is always good to have a white man around, it allays suspicion.' (74) Brenda, similarly, observes: 'Evidence from a white man will carry enormous weight.' (115)

Racial discrimination is assaulted in passage after passage. One of the most elaborate is on pages 5–9, when Moses is playing with the fact that black people in London often work on night shift.

If it is too much to ask the sightseer or daytime Londoner to rise and shine ere crack o'dawn for the sight of a spade, there is another time when he can satisfy his curiosity. He has only to wait for the knell of midnight or thereabouts when the civilized world is in bed or about to hit the hay for the stalwart blacks to come tumbling out of the ghettoes.

Once again, the city is in their hands. (8)

By opposing 'the civilized world' to 'the stalwart blacks', it is implied, with due irony, that civilization must be white. The whole novel is largely a response to the assumption that the culture of Europeans is superior to the culture of others, whether Africans, Asians or Caribbean people.

It often confutes or redirects offensive stereotypes. 'Smelling them basement smells as they combine with Galahad sour sweat, remind me of the fable that English people broadcast that we smell more than them', a telling passage begins. (79) Immediately we are offered a tour of filthy English habits. Of a white man who cannot read, the sarcastic Brenda remarks: 'He is illiterate, but being as he's white we say he is suffering from dyslexia.' (128)

According to Moses, 'English people so stupid that the whole lot of Orientals and Blacks is the same kettle of fish as far as they are concerned.' (51) But he himself, parody of an English landlord, finds it difficult to distinguish one Indian from another. Accepting illegal immigrants, he pleads:

...when it is after midnight and you are in London, a civilized capital metropolis where you do not expect such things to happen – need I go on, dear R? Can you blame me for my tremulous voice and my hollow laughter? Can you blame me if I saw this cluster of beings as in a blur, unable to distinguish one from the other? (72)

Though critical of the English, Moses tends to identify with English manners, even to the point of what in *The Lonely Londoners* is called 'the old diplomacy'.[7] 'I asked Galahad if he'd like a cup of tea – politeness and genteelity being the only counter for such as my present guest...' (11) His initial response when Faizull proposes to slaughter a sheep in the garden is stereotypically English: 'I'm afraid it's out of the question,' he says. Though tempted by an opportunity for 'research', he objects: 'This is very unusual. What will the neighbours say?' (50)

At least as important in this novel as the many points made about social and racial attitudes is the running commentary on Trying To Be An Author. Moses is all for 'writing Literature', (103) 'showing the white people that we, too, could write book.' (101) Moses is a writer with whose problems Selvon, at a safe ironic distance, can often identify. 'What do you know of the deep maelstroms churning inside an author, or how *touchous* he could be concerning his work?' (108)

Selvon's major contribution to Caribbean fiction in English has been to mould a literary version of Trinidad speech and – as V.S. Reid had done with Jamaican in *New Day* (1949) – to employ the creole not in dialogue only but also as the language of narration. In the words of Selvon himself, he 'modified the dialect, keeping the lilt and rhythm.'[8] In a more recent interview he adds: 'I saw potential in this modified dialect to the extent that in my last novel using this language form, *Moses Ascending*, I experimented even further with using both this and an archaic form of English which is not spoken anywhere today.'[9]

The characteristic effects of *Moses Ascending* (as of *Moses Migrating*)[10] derive from the surprising combination of styles: archaic and modern; formal, often stilted, Standard English and casual Trinidad slang, academic phraseology and non-Standard grammar; pseudo-literary affectations, clichés, foreign expressions, all tumbled together with splendid indecorum, and the detail often wrong. 'I will knock them in the Old Kent Road with my language alone,' boasts Moses. 'My very usage of English will have them rolling in the aisles.' (78) The literary burlesque is enriched by a range of reference as varied as the style: there are allusions to English classics, Greek mythology, Trinidad calypso, international pop songs, Roman history, British Empire history, Trinidad carnival, the titles of novels or films, and so on – as Moses, with grandiloquent aplomb, displays his cultural store.

Throughout the novel, Moses struggles with his 'magnus opus' (103), The Memoirs he evidently considers *de rigueur* for the man of property he thinks he has become. Moses, scribbling away up in his 'penthouse', in (so to speak) the private tower of his imagination, is confronted by Galahad, a prescriptive critic. For Galahad, a real writer needs to be in the thick of things. 'How you expect to stay lock up in your room, and don't go and investigate and do research, and take part in what is happening, and write book?' (43) Moses, persuaded of the need for 'topicality and subjects of interest' (63), starts carrying a clipboard for note-taking, and frequently claims to be in pursuit of material; steaming open other people's letters 'for the sake of...research' (60), getting caught up in Black Power activity 'through researching for [his] Memoirs.' (98) We may believe that, unlike Brenda, we never see the Memoirs; or we may conclude, on the implications of the final page, that Moses' Memoirs are the book we have been reading. Whatever we decide, it would seem – from Brenda's comments and from the hilariously hybrid nature of his discourse in the novel – that Moses' Memoirs are a hodge-podge of registers. Brenda, a formalist critic, takes apart the style.

> The only sentence you know, Moses...is what criminals get. Your conjunctions and your hyperboles are all mixed up with your syntax, and your figures of speech only fall between 10 and 20. Where you have punctuation you should have allegory and predicates, so that the pronouns appear in the correct context. In other words, you should stick to oral communication and leave the written word to them what knows their business. (104–5)

Brenda's comment itself, of course, enacts incompetence. Sentence (as in grammar) becomes sentence (as in law court); figures (as in rhetoric) become figures (as in arithmetic); jargon words from grammar and literary criticism – 'conjunctions', 'hyperboles', 'syntax', 'punctuation', 'allegory', 'predicates', 'pronouns' – are thrown together ridiculously; though the structure suggests a reasoned judgement, particularly in the academic tone, the pseudo-logical clarity, of: 'where you have... you should have..., so that the... appear in the correct context.' 'Correct' (for proper) sounds slightly odd, as is appropriate here. Exhorting Moses to be correct, Brenda caps it all by being ungrammatical herself, counselling that he '...leave the written word to them what knows their business.'

Them what knows their business, Selvon gently indicates, are not only the authors of England, but also reputable Black Writers such as James Baldwin, George Lamming and Andrew Salkey: all three are committed in a way that recommends them to Galahad and the group down in the basement; and all three write elegant Standard English. Repeated mention of James

Baldwin, and *The Fire Next Time*,[11] connects the problems of blacks in Britain with problems in America, and reinforces the link between the American BP and Galahad, Brenda and company. Lamming and Salkey are named partly because they are friends of the author, Selvon, and their literary/political attitudes differ somewhat from his. The references are among the literary in-jokes with which *Moses Ascending* is replete, a sort of affectionate teasing and some free advertisement. 'You think writing book is like kissing hand? You should leave that to people like Lamming and Salkey.' (42) Talk (mostly by Galahad) of 'My People' or 'Our People' seems to echo Lamming's Trumper in *In the Castle of My Skin*; Trumper who at the end of that novel, on his return to Creighton village from the United States, tells – boasts, really – of his commitment to black solidarity. Similarly, Moses' judgement that Brenda's 'tone of voice indicated that she was aroused, and England expects every man to do his duty' (25) winks at a passage in Lamming's *Castle*:[12]

> 'How do you know nothing will happen?' the girl said. She was anxious.
> 'England expects every man to know his duty,' the male voice said. 'Come close.'

At the welcome-home party for Bob, Moses sneers at the assembly of black ticket-holders and gate-crashers: 'this is rather a riff-raff lot,' he complains to Brenda. 'Couldn't you of asked Lamming and Salkey and some of their English contemporaries?' (120) At the end of the book we see Moses, down in the basement room to which he has descended, 'kicking aside a batch of Lamming's *Water For Berries*'. (138) Moses gets the title comically wrong. *Water With Berries*,[13] the book being kicked aside, is a novel concerned, like *Moses Ascending*, with the Caribbean would-be artist in London; and the title, from Shakespeare's *The Tempest*, signals versions of Caliban. (In the Selvon novel the surprising response of an Asian to whom Moses, the landlord, says 'Speakee English?' (69) is a parody illustration of Caliban's 'You taught me language; and my profit on't/ Is, I know how to curse…')[14]

xiii

The Prospero-Caliban paradigm of the colonial relationship – Caliban is resentful – is less important in *Moses Ascending* than the Crusoe-Friday. *Moses Ascending*, like Derek Walcott's play *Pantomime* (first performed in 1978),[15] inverts the Crusoe-Friday model: black Moses has a white 'man Friday' (4, 102). Selvon toys with the notion that the 'man-Friday' is an 'immigrant' (4) from 'the Black Country' (31), the English Midlands. The Selvon parody is not merely general; there are moments when he seems to have in mind specific passages in *Robinson Crusoe*. Look, for example, at the following brief excerpts from the Defoe:[16]

'I…taught him to say Master, and then let him know, that was to be my name…' (p.209)

'I found Friday…was still a cannibal in his nature; but I discovered [revealed] so much abhorrence at the very thoughts of it, and at the least appearance of it, that he durst not discover it…' (p.210)

'…never man had a more faithful, loving, sincere servant, than Friday was to me; without passions, sullenness, or designs, perfectly obliged and engaged…' (p.211)

'This frequently gave me occasion to observe, and that with wonder, that … God, in His providence … has bestowed upon them the same powers, the same reason, the same affections, the same sentiments of kindness and obligation, the same passions and resentments of wrongs, the same sense of gratitude, sincerity, fidelity, and all the capacities of doing good and receiving good, that He has given to us…' (p.212)

'I was greatly delighted with him, and made it my business to teach him every thing that was proper to make him useful, handy, and helpful…' (p.213)

'I seriously prayed to God that He would enable me to instruct savingly this poor savage…and would guide me to speak so to him from the word of God, as his conscience might be convinced, his eyes opened, and his soul saved.' (p.221)

From the Selvon novel, here is Moses talking about Bob:

> He was a willing worker, eager to learn the ways of the Black man. In no time at all he learn how to cook peas and rice and to make a beef stew... As we became good friends, or rather Master and Servant, I try to convert him from the evils of alcohol, but it was no use. By and by, as he was so useful to me, I allowed him the freedom of the house, and left everything in his hands so I could enjoy my retirement.
>
> And whilst I was indoctrinating him, I also learn a lesson myself, which is that Black and White could live in harmony, for he was loyal and true, and never listened to all that shit you hear about black people. Afterwards he tell me he used to believe it, but since coming under my employ he realize that black people is human too.
>
> I decided to teach him the Bible when I could make the time. (4–5)

Moses is presented as aware of the original Crusoe-Friday relationship; but it is with Selvon (beyond Moses) that we share the parodic detail. First person narration does, of course, encourage this sort of irony. The author knows and understands much more than Moses does. 'Selvon,' Michel Fabre has written, 'does not assimilate into the European mainstream; he explodes it, he subverts it... This is really a "novelist's novel", refined to the point of indulging in pun, parody and allusion in the same breath.'[17]

'Mark my words,' advises Moses. (78) When, for example, he says 'I had to *peddle* my own canoe for survival' (39), Moses no doubt means 'paddle'. There is a glance at Mr Biswas, 'the paddler'.[18] 'Peddle' suggests that the writer, however independent he pretends to be, will need people to buy his work. It may also signal an upper class English pronunciation of 'paddle'. Similarly, when Moses says, 'In this world you must not *heng* your hat too high' (3), 'heng' simultaneously represents a version of upper class English speech and a West Indian Creole usage: thus neatly fusing dream and reality. Moses, so often critical of others, is frequently exposed by his own narration. He exemplifies – hugely exaggerated – tendencies that do exist.[19] He is a

West Indian immigrant acculturated to a British life-style; and 'his language,' Maureen Warner-Lewis has observed, 'will reflect the temptations and perils of any acculturation process through its bizarre juxtapositions and comic excesses, through Moses' synthesis of popular and formal cultures, and of his semi-literacy and book learning.'[20]

Primarily, however, I see Moses as a set of attitudes affording Selvon some well taken opportunities for literary burlesque, for provoking laughter against snobbery, racism, deceit; against English assumptions of superiority; against people – often Caribbean people – who would prescribe how writers should work; against people – including Caribbean people – who are slow to value anything outside the mainstream of traditional English Literature.

MERVYN MORRIS
Department of English,
University of the West Indies,
Kingston 7, Jamaica.

Notes

1. *Moses Ascending* (London: Davis-Poynter, 1975). *The Lonely Londoners* (London: Alan Wingate, 1956; Longman, 1972). Other books by Selvon (published in London): *A Brighter Sun* (Alan Wingate, 1952), *An Island Is A World* (Alan Wingate, 1955), *Ways of Sunlight* (MacGibbon and Kee, 1957), *Turn Again Tiger* (MacGibbon and Kee, 1958; Heinemann, 1979), *I Hear Thunder* (MacGibbon and Kee, 1963), *The Housing Lark* (MacGibbon and Kee, 1965), *A Drink of Water*, for children (1968), *The Plains of Caroni* (MacGibbon and Kee, 1970) and *Those Who Eat the Cascadura* (Davis-Poynter, 1972). For an excellent brief account of Selvon's fiction, see: 'Samuel Selvon' by Michel Fabre, in Bruce King (ed.), *West Indian Literature* (London: Macmillan, 1979).
2. Page references to *Moses Ascending* given as numbers after each quotation.
3. 'In Moses' unconscious blunders...Selvon's conscious artistry...': Edward Baugh, 'Friday in Crusoe's City: the Question of Lan-

guage in Two West Indian Novels of Exile', in Helen Tiffin (ed.), *ACLALS Bulletin* Fifth Series No. 3 (Queensland: December 1980), p.10. The article reappears in Satendra Nandan (ed.), *Language and Literature in Multicultural Contexts*, ACLALS Fifth Triennial Conference Proceedings (Suva: University of the South Pacific and ACLALS, 1983), which also includes a sustained comparison of *The Lonely Londoners* and *Moses Ascending*: Victor Ramraj, 'Selvon's Londoners: From the Centre to the Periphery'.

4. *The Lonely Londoners* (Longman edition), p.122.
5. Ibid. p.124.
6. 'Stokely Carmichael, the Trinidadian-born American Black Power leader visited London and magnetized a whole set of splintered feelings that had for a long time been seeking a union. Carmichael enunciated a way of seeing the black West Indian that seemed to many to make sense of the entire history of slavery and colonial suppression, of the African diaspora into the New World. And he gave it a name.' Edward Brathwaite, in 'Timehri', *Savacou* No.2 (Kingston, September 1970), p.40.
7. See, for example. *The Lonely Londoners* (Longman edition) p.24 and p.47.
8. Selvon interviewed by Michel Fabre, London, 11 November, 1977. Quoted by Michel Fabre in Bruce King (ed.), *West Indian Literature*; p.117. See also Michel Fabre, 'Moses And The Queen's English', *Trinidad and Tobago Review* Vol.4 No.4, Christmas 1980, p.13.
9. 'Samuel Selvon Talking: A Conversation with Kenneth Ramchand', *Canadian Literature* No. 95 (Vancouver, Winter 1982), pp.60–1. See also Peter Nazareth, 'Interview with Sam Selvon', *World Literature Written in English*, Vol. 18 No. 2 (Guelph: November 1979), pp. 422–3.
10. London: Longman, 1983.
11. First published 1963.
12. George Lamming, *In the Castle of My Skin*, (London: Michael Joseph, 1953). Longman edition, 1970, p.177.
13. George Lamming, *Water With Berries* (London: Longman, 1971).
14. William Shakespeare, *The Tempest* I ii 363–5.
15. Published 1980 (with *Remembrance*).
16. Daniel Defoe, *Robinson Crusoe* (Penguin English Library edition, 1965).
17. Bruce King (ed.), *West Indian Literature*, pp.123–4. Also in *Trinidad and Tobago Review* Vol.4 No.4 (Port of Spain, Christmas 1980), p.15.

18. V.S. Naipaul, *A House for Mr Biswas* (London: André Deutsch, 1961); p.265, for example.

19. 'This style is humorous because of its apparently incongruous juxtapositions. But the incongruity is only apparent. It is true to the life of modern colonized man...': Peter Nazareth, 'The Clown in the Slave Ship', *Caribbean Quarterly* Vol. 23 Nos. 2 & 3 (Kingston: June–September 1977), p. 24.

20. Maureen Warner-Lewis, 'Samuel Selvon's Linguistic Extravaganza: *Moses Ascending*', conference paper, May 1982, University of the West Indies, Mona, Jamaica, p.3.

It was Sir Galahad who drew my attention to the property. He was reading *Dalton's Weekly*, as was his wont, looking for new jobs; roaming through bedsitter land; picking out secondhand miscellany he need and could afford; musing on the lonely hearts column to see if any desperate rich white woman seeks black companion with a view to matrimony; and speculating when he come to the properties-for-sale page, buying houses and renovating them to sell and make big profit.

Little did he dream that whilst he dreamt I was on the lookout for an investment in truth.

'Hello Moses!' he say, stretching the pages out and backing the one with the item he was reading. 'Tolroy's property is up for sale. Listen to this: "Highly desirable mansion in exclusive part of Shepherd's Bush. Vacant possession. Owner migrating to Jamaica. Viewing strictly by appointment with agent." That's Tolroy's house. It got his address.'

'Does it say how much he's asking?' I ask.

'No. He'll be lucky if he could give it away. You never seen it?'

'No, you?'

'Yes. You ever build houses with playing cards when you was a little boy?'

'Yeah.'

'And you shift one card and the whole house collapse?'

'Yeah.'

'That's Tolroy's mansion.'

Nevertheless Galahad didn't know one arse about houses; it's true some of these terraces in London look like they might capsize any minute, but united we stand, divided we fall, and knowing Tolroy as I do, it stand to reason that he would not of bought no end-of-terrace house, but one plunk in the middle what would have support on both sides.

True enough it turned out when I went to see it and get some more details from Tolroy, such as it had a five-year lease, two of which was gone, and it was due for LCC demolition. It sounded like the sort of thing I could afford.

'That's why it's going so cheap, Moses,' Tolroy say. 'If you let out rooms you can make your money back in no time at all. Besides, you will be a landlord and not a tenant.'

It was this latter point which decided me in the end. After all these years paying rent, I had the ambition to own my own property in London, no matter how ruinous or dilapidated it was. If you are a tenant, you catch your arse forever, but if you are a landlord, it is a horse of a different colour. Take the HP, for instance:

'Er, Mr Moses, er, I'm sorry about this procedure, but we usually ask if our customers know anyone who will be prepared to act as a guarantor? Perhaps your landlord?'

'I beg your pardon, *I* am the landlord.'

'Oh … how silly of me … if you'll just sign the form here, SIR … sit down … use my chair.'

I can also be on the other side of the door when people come to look for rooms.

'Is the landlord in?'

'*I* am the landlord.'

'Oh … I'm looking for a room.'

'I don't let out to black people.'

SLAM.

I might even qualify for jury service.

'I hereby deem you a rogue and a vagabond. You will go to jail, you worthless scamp, and await Her Majesty's pleasure.'

These are only some of the privileges that would be mine.

'I tell you, boy Moses,' Tolroy say, 'if I wasn't *immigrading* I wouldn't of sell. And as it's you, I will forget all the other buyers who are eager and give you priority.' He take a deep breath, like a poker player about to put down a royal flush, and say, 'You will even be zero-rated for VAT.'

I don't want you to think that it was Tolroy's spiel what inveigle me; I did already make up my mind.

When Galahad get wind of what I was about he rub his hands together.

'When do we take possession?' he ask.

'This is the parting of the ways,' I tell him. 'You can have this whole basement room to yourself. When I leave here, my past

2

will be behind me, you inclusive.'

I knew he would take it as a joke though I mean it in serious.

'You can't erase me like that,' he say, 'I am part and parcel of your life.'

'I have trained you for the London jungle, Galahad,' I tell him, 'and from now on you are on your own.'

'I suppose you going to live in that whole house by yourself,' he sneer.

'I'll have tenants,' I say, 'but you won't be one of them.'

'We shall see who needs who,' he say, 'I have noticed that you look as if you ready to retire, but I am with it, man. You will need me to cope with current events and the new generation of black people.'

'That's where you wrong,' I say. 'I just want to live in peace, and reap the harvest of the years of slavery I put in in Brit'n. I don't want people like you around, to upset the apple cart.'

'I won't beg you to take me,' he say, 'but watch out. The old days are finished. It is a new era. And old-timers like you will be just brushed aside.'

'There's nothing more I'd rather,' I say sincerely. 'You may visit when you feel like it, but remember your station. There will be no more bonhomie 'tween us.'

I do not think that Galahad took me serious then, nor at any other time. When people come to expect a certain pattern of behaviour from you, they refuse to accept that a man could change, and turn over a new leaf. But I did not give two hoots for Sir Galahad.

To cut a long story short, I clinch the deal with Tolroy. In this world you must not *heng* your hat too high. I would naturally of preferred a mansion in Belgravia or a penthouse in Mayfair, without too many black people around, but I had the feeling that if I didn't make the move now, I would be doomed to the basement brigade for the rest of my life.

Having lived below the surface of the world all my life I ensconced myself in the highest flat in the house: if it had an attic I might of even gone higher still. It had a tall London plane what growing outside, and one of the branches stretch near the window. I would of prefer if it was a mango tree, or a calabash, to remind me of home, but you can't have everything. Also, being

3

at the top of all them stairs was a deterrent to idlers and hustlers calling too frequently.

I cannot tell you what joy and satisfaction I had the day I move into these new quarters. Whereas I did have a worm's eye view of life, I now had a bird's eye view. I was Master of the house. I insert my key in the front door lock, I enter, I ascend the stairs, and when the tenants hear my heavy tread they cower and shrink in their rooms, in case I snap my fingers and say OUT to any of them.

What a change it was to go and put up notices of vacancies on the hoardings, instead of reading them myself to find a place to live! And I record with pride that I wasn't one of them prejudiced landlord what put No Kolors on their notices. Come one, come all, first come, first served, was my mottos. It was also my policy to avoid any petty restrictions for the tenants who was giving me my bread. Live and let live was another motto, as long as every Friday-please-God they shell over their respective rents, and didn't grumble too much about leaks and cracks and other symptoms of dilapidation which infested the house.

The only thing I didn't want was to have any of the old brigade living in my house, and the rumour went around town that I was a different man, that I had forsaken my friends, and that there was no more pigfoot and peas and rice, nor even a cuppa, to be obtained, even if they came with gifts of myrrh and frankincense.

All these arrangements were attended to by my man Friday, a white immigrant name Bob from somewhere in the Midlands, who came to seek his fortunes in London. My blood take him because he was a good worker, young and strong and he put down three weeks' rent in advance. By the time the three weeks was up he was spitting and polishing all over the house, tearing down old wallpaper and putting up new ones, painting and puttying, sweeping and scrubbing. He was a willing worker, eager to learn the ways of the Black man. In no time at all he learn how to cook peas and rice and to make a beef stew. I got him cracking because he didn't have no more money to pay rent, and we come to an agreement for him to be my batman and to attend to all the petty details about running the house in lieu. He arrive with a big crate full of comic books and was forever thumbing through them and leaving them all about the place.

4

The only thing I didn't like about him was he went out most evenings and come back pissed, drunk like a lord. As we became good friends, or rather Master and Servant, I try to convert him from the evils of alcohol, but it was no use. By and by, as he was so useful to me, I allowed him the freedom of the house, and left everything in his hands so I could enjoy my retirement.

And whilst I was indoctrinating him, I also learn a lesson myself, which is that Black and White could live in harmony, for he was loyal and true, and never listened to all that shit you hear about black people. Afterwards he tell me he used to believe it, but since coming under my employ he realize that black people is human too.

I decided to teach him the Bible when I could make the time.

▲ ▲ ▲ ▲

As soon as I had explained his duties to Bob and he took the responsibilities off my shoulders, I relaxed and started to work on my Memoirs. One of the things that gave me great delight was to be able to stay in bed and think of all them hustlers who had to get up and go to work. At first this gave me a selfish pleasure, but then I got to taking an objective view of this whole business of employment.

Sometimes in the winter when the alarm go and you get up and look through the window to see the weather conditions and you can't see nothing, only smog and frost out there, and the sky so grey and gloomy it look as if it join-up with the earth and make one, you does wonder what crime this country commit that it have to punish so with this evil weather. It is not the alarm what really wake you up: it is cold in your arse.

The alarms of all the black people in Brit'n are timed to ring before the rest of the population. It is their destiny to be up and about at the crack o'dawn. In these days of pollution and environment, he is very lucky, for he can breathe the freshest air of the new day before anybody else. He does not know how fortunate he is. He does not know how privileged he is to be in charge of the city whilst the rest of Brit'n is still abed. He strides the streets, he is Manager of all the offices in *Threadaneedle*

5

street, he is Chief Executive of London Transport and British Railways, he is Superintendent of all the hospitals, he is Landlord of all the mansions in Park Lane and Hampstead, he is Head Gourmet and Master Chef of all the restaurants. He ain't reach the stage yet of scrubbing the floors of Buckingham Palace or captaining the heads therein. There is a scramble among the rest of the loyal population for these royal jobs, but with time, he too might be exalted to these ranks – who knows?

Instead of moaning and groaning about his sorrows, he should stop and think and count these blessings reserved solely for him. He should realize that if wasn't for him, the city would go on sleeping forever. He should look upon himself as a pioneer what preparing the way for the city's day, polishing the brass and chrome, washing the pots and pans. As he banishes the filth and litter, he could thunder out decrees in the Houses of Parliament and his voice would ring through the corridors and change the Immigration Act and the policies of the Racial Board.

What is that heavy footfall on the cold damp pavement before the rest of the world is awake? What is that freezing figure fumbling through the fog, feeling its way to the bus stop, or clattering down the steps of the sleepy underground at this unearthly hour?

It is the black man. He is the first passenger of the day. He is the harbinger who will put the kettle on to boil. He holds the keys of the city, and he will unlock the doors and tidy the papers on the desk, flush the loo, straighten the chairs, hoover the carpet. He will press switches and start motors. He will empty dustbins and ashtrays and stack boxes. He will peel the spuds. He will sweep the halls and grease the engines.

As he stands, mayhap, in some wall-to-wall carpeted mansion (resting, dreaming on his broom or hoover) and looks about him at mahogany furniture, at deeply-padded sofas and armchairs, at myriading chandeliers, at hi-fi set and colour television, as his eyes roam on leather-bound tomes and velvet curtains and cushions, at silver cutlery and crystal glass, at Renoirs and Van Goghs and them other fellars, what thoughts of humble gratitude should go through his mind! Here he is, monarch of all he surveys, passing the wine, toasting the Queen, carving the baron of beef, perambulating among distinguished guests, pausing,

6

perhaps, for a word on the fluctuation of gilt-edge shares or the new play in the West End.

And the black man is the chosen race to dream such dreams, and to enjoy the splendour and the power whilst the whole rest of the world still in slumberland!

Oh, the ingratitude, the unreasonableness of those who only see one side of the coin, and complain that he is given only the menial tasks to perform!

(As I became objective, I was mad to jump up and put on my clothes and go straight to work!)

Consider him standing too, in Regent street of a cold winter's morn, leaning on his refuse cart, a lone, commanding figure, directing the arterial flow of the traffics as thousands of vehicles ply hither and thither, to and yon. Who was it but one of these solitaires who suggested the brilliant idea to London Transport to divert the buses–them in the heart of Piccadilly Circus, thus alleviating chaos and confusion for millions?

Great thoughts does come to men when the world is hushed and is foreday morning.

Strangers to London – even bona fide Londoners too – have been heard to remark that they can't see the hordes of black faces what supposed to clutter the vast metropolis. Ah, but at what time of the day do they make this observation? If they had to get their arses out of a warm bed in the wee hours, if they had to come out of cosy flat and centrally-heated hallways to face the onslaught of an icy north wind and trudge through the sludge and grime of a snow-trampled pavement, they would encounter black man and woman by the thousands.

There is no dearth ere dawn. The first flake of snow in the winter falls on a black man. The first ray of sunlight in the summer falls on a black man. The first yellow leaf in the autumn falls on a black man. The first crocus in the spring is seen by a black man, and he harks to the cuckoo long before all them other people what write to the newspapers to say they was the first.

Is it too dear a price to pay for these pleasures that gladden the heart and lift the spirits? And to augment the argument, is it nothing that the black man has a monopoly on these pristine delights?

Fie, I say, on those who look on one side of the coin alone.

7

God's blood, things have come to a pretty pass when in the midst of the trials and tribulations that are his lot, he is displeased when he is put to manage the fair city, and can make or break the tenor of the day for some Very Important Person merely by puting an ashtray in its right place, or straightening the blotting pad on a desk!

If it is too much to ask the sightseer or daytime Londoner to rise and shine ere crack o'dawn for the sight of a spade, there is another time when he can satisfy his curiosity. He has only to wait for the knell of midnight or thereabouts when the civilized world is in bed or about to hit the hay for the stalwart blacks to come tumbling out of the ghettoes.

Once again, the city is in their hands. It is not beyond speculation to imagine that it might well of been a black man who wrote those immortal words: '... but they, while their companions slept, were toiling upward in the night.' For indeed, the duties of the night is another monopoly granted to him for his love and devotion to labour.

Thus, he not only has one monopoly. He has *two*. And yet he complains!

If to say this country was invaded in the night when everybody sleeping, who would raise the alarm but one of these nocturnal toilers struggling through a bitter nor'-nor'-easterly on his way to factory or station, who would instantly forget his own miseries and dial 999?

Again, it is not too far-fetched as some might think, that it might of been a black man what pen them famous words: 'The darkies (sic) watch of the night is the one before dawn, and relief is often nearest us when we least expect it.'

When you consider the working hours of the spade, is it any wonder that the few who are on the scene in normal course of the day appear bleary-eyed and dopey? This is the explanation, not drugs nor all-night parties. When you see them on the last train or the first bus, it is not homeward angel after revelry and debauchery, it is action stations they are bound for.

There is one last point which will illustrate how ungrateful the wretches are. Not only do they hold the exclusive charter for those peaceful working watches when they can avoid the rush hour as millions of white mice dart to and fro, but *they are*

8

actually paid higher wages than if they worked in daylight!

Really and truly, the profound observation that life is a funny thing is a great thought, for with all these advantages, he still moans and groans that he is unfairly treated, when in truth and in fact the boot is on the other foot.

The population masses believe that racial violence going to erupt because he is being continuously and continually oppressed and kept down. Not so.

It is true that racial violence going to erupt, but not for that reason. What going to happen is one of these days the white man going to realize that the black man have it cushy, being as he got the whole day to do what he like, hustle pussy or visit the museums and the historical buildings, what remain open to facilitate him (yet another boon) and close-up the moment that he, the white man, left work. Furthermore, he will begin to suspect that it must be have some attraction, else why would all them spades clamour for employment in such evil hours?

Last, but not least, he will realize that the formation of that valiant and glorious group called The Black Watch wasn't by accident, that the black man is already earmarked and commemorated in history.

As the truth dawn (as it were) the white man will not only grit his teeth in envy, rage and frustration. It is *then* that he will erupt and kick up RASS!

You can see, from that dissertation, that I was already reaping the benefits of my retirement, for how can such astute observations come to a man unless his mind be at peace, and he does not have to worry about going to work? And believe me, I know what I am talking about. I can justifiably claim to be more knowledgeable than most when it come to working evil hours, for it was not by winning the pools, nor spotting the missing ball, that I came into the fortune to buy the house. It was by the sweat of my brow, so do not jealous me, dear R, now that I can afford a few little luxuries, such as having a white man as my au pair. It distresses me sometimes when I see how some men squander their lives in Brit'n, and have nothing to show for their years of toil, be it ever so humble as my penthouse in Shepherd's Bush. Where have they gone? What are they doing? Somewhere out there, somewhere among the millions of whites; in the bustling traffics and the towering buildings and the confusion and pandemonium of the city, they are scattered and lost. I only hear stories of their plights and sorrows, tales of tragedy whispered on the wind. I hear that Big City has gone mad, walks about the streets muttering to himself, ill-kempt and unshaven, and does not recognize anyone. It is as if the whole city of London collapse on him, as if the pressures build up until he could stand it no more and had was to make a wild dash around the bend. Some, I hear, have migrated to the North, to Birmingham and Manchester and Leeds, to try their luck, and I wish them well. Others have gone back to the islands, and God alone knows what happening to them down there, as they went with white wives, and that is the greatest tragedy of all, as apart from mosquito bite, there are other kinds of mosquito who want to have a bite of white pussy too.

If you do not keep in touch with your friends and acquaintances you will think they are *dead* in this country. They vanish from your life; they go down in the underground and they never emerge; they are blurred into a crowd and become part of the density of humanity, individualistic only in a kind of limbo memory.

As I settled down into my new life I was sometimes tempted to try and trace their whereabouts, but prudence prevailed, for I know, that wherever they are, there would be a lurch, and they would want me to pull them out of it.

Of course, Galahad did not include himself as an undesirable, and having waited a decent interval for me to get organized, he made himself my first visitor.

He arrived in his Black Power glad rags. Starting from foot to head, he have on a pair of platforms, yellow socks, purple corduroy trousers, a leather belt about six inches broad with a big heavy brass buckle and some fancy, spiky chunks of metal studded in it ('That's my weapon. Look.' He haul the belt right out of the loops and wield it like a Viking. 'I will slaughter a white man one day.') He have on a pink shirt. On both hands, he had on a battery of chunky signet rings, wearing them on unconventional digits. Round his neck he had a heavy chain like what peasants in Trinidad tether their cattle with. And on top of his head, he had on a navy-blue wool cap, pulled down over his ears.

When I opened the door Galahad raise his right hand up in the air making a fist of his fingers as if he going to bust a cuff in my arse, and say, paradoxically, 'Peace, brother. Black is beautiful.'

'Is that you, Galahad?' I ask, backing off from the cuff he was threatening me with.

'It sure is.' He come in and start to model. 'How you like the rags, man? You dig, or you don't dig?'

'Way out, man,' I say.

'That's cool,' he say. 'I am glad to see you in prosperous surroundings. It is good for Our People to make progress. But you must not forget the struggle.'

'I'm glad you appreciate that I struggled to get where I am,' I say.

'Not that struggle,' he wave my words away. 'I mean *the* struggle. It is only right that you should contribute to the cause. We need financiers. Without the black gentry and nobility on our side, it is a losing battle.'

'I didn't know a battle was going on,' I say.

'Ah!' he wag a finger at me. 'You start already to deny your countrymen! As soon as a black man start to get out of the ghetto and into the castle, he turn a blind eye to the struggle. You are not going to join that band of traitors? We have enough of them to contend with.'

Bob came in unobtrusively and enquired whether I needed anything further for the evening, as he was going out to get pissed. I asked Galahad if he'd like a cup of tea – politeness and genteelity being the only counter for such as my present guest – and he wanted to know if we didn't have anything stronger.

'A sherry, perhaps? Bob offered.

'Don't give him my sherry, Bob,' I tell him. 'Tea's good enough for the likes of him.'

'Oh. One of those, eh?' Bob say, and went off dutifully to make the brew.

You see how good I had him trained already?

'Who's he?' Galahad ask.

'My best friend and ally,' I say.

'H'mm.' But he was not to be distracted from his course. He start the rap again. 'We are all in the same boat. You can buy a house or a limousine, and eat caviar and best end of lamb, but

11

you can't get a white skin if you beg, borrow or steal. Things not like the old days, Moses.'

'You telling me,' I say.

'The revolution has come. At last the Black man is coming into his own.'

'Exactly,' I say. 'I am coming into my own, and I just want to be left in peace.'

'You don't understand.' Galahad shake his head as if he sorry for me. 'The time is ripe now. Long ago we had to stand up and take the blows, but these days we have a chance to fight back. Black Power! All over the world the cry is going up. Power to the people!' And he lift his hand and make that threatening gesture again, as if he want to thump me one.

'Save all your steam and energy for Hyde Park Corner,' I say.

'You can contribute,' he say, 'we need money badly.'

'That's your problem.'

'Correction. It is *our* problem. You can't sit on the fence. Those who are not for us are against us. Stand up and be counted. Moses! When the revolution moves,' he went on, 'the first to go will be those like you who refuse to live with the times. When I first come to Brit'n you was a different man, Moses. You was like a leader, and all the boys would listen to your advice.'

'Just cool it, man.' I was getting a bit fed up.

'I have to get through to you,' he say. 'It is my duty. If I got to spend the whole night here, I have to communicate. One of our troubles is that we don't talk enough, but I am going to convince you if it's the last thing I do.'

All the time Galahad was walking up and down as he rap, flinging his hands in the air, and every now and then a fleck of spit flying out of his mouth which I dodge when I see it coming. When Black Power come into vogue Galahad was one of the first to rally to the colours – I mean colour, of course. An American visitor from the Deep South indoctrinate him, and he became a rabid disciple, calling everybody Brother and Sister and advising them to change their names from Churchill or ffoulkes-Sutherland to Obozee or Fadghewi or some other African names what I can't spell. He form up a Party in Ladbroke Grove and start to fight oppression and all the other ills that beset black people.

'I will come to the point.' he say.

'Do,' I say.

'We want to bring out a newspaper,' he say. 'You know these English papers does only have contorted views of the scene. If we get our own, we can tell the people the truth.'

'I will buy a copy when you bring it out,' I say.

Bob return with the tea, placed the tray on the table, collected a couple of comic books he had lying around, and withdrew.

'Ah well,' Galahad shrug and being to sip his cup. 'Maybe some other time when you in a better mood I can tap you for some new pence.' He change the topic. 'I glad you get a house at last, boy. I don't suppose you got a room to spare?'

'Not for you,' I tell him. 'And in any case, Bob attends to the running of the house. I leave everything up to him.'

'Tut, tut. Like prosperity gone to your head.'

'My pocket, too. And it's staying there.'

'If I didn't know you well, Moses, you would fool me. But I know you only saying that, and you would ease-up your countrymen whenever you could.'

'Try me.'

'Don't worry, I know you will rally to the cause in the long run. We compiling a list, you know. We putting down all those that we can depend on, and all those who are not reliable. We weeding out the sheeps from the goats.'

He finished his tea and walk to the door. He stand up there and once more make a fist in the air.

'Black is beautiful. Power to the people!'

'We shall overcome!' I cry, returning his salute at the last minute, as I didn't want him hanging around, and thinking that this last gesture would spur his exit, and also defend me in case of surprise attack. 'We is we!' he say, as an MP culminating his speech to the House of Commons dramatically, 'and after we, is weevil!'

▲ ▲ ▲ ▲

Thoughts filled me when Galahad left. I smoothed the pages of my Memoirs, and am giving it to you sic, as I intend to do as long as I can – how much faithful can I be? You have it straight from the horse's mouth. The thoughts that fill me was thoughts about how a man could wish he is just living his life, and how people want you to become involve, whether you want to or not. You just cannot live your own life and do the things you want to. I didn't have anything to do with black power, nor white power, nor any fucking power but my own. Why it is that a man can't make his own decisions, and live in peace without all this interference? It is enough trouble for me to cogitate on the very fact of being alive in this world, wondering what going to happen to me, if when I dead I going to come back alive again, if it have a heaven which part milk and honey flow, and if it have a hell where you have to stoke the coals all the time to keep the fires going, else you end up like those favourite English cartoons of a white man hanging by his thumbs against a wall, or in a desert, with all his footprints behind him, panting for water. These are shuddering thoughts: it is enough to fill your brains for the rest of your life. Yet men would come and ask you if you voting, or if you going to contribute, or if you going to join the rally in Trafalgar Square and march with the masses to number ten Downing street. Suppose, just suppose, that you don't want to do any of them fucking things – you don't want to join no club, you don't want to rocket to the moon, you don't want to cross the Atlantic single-handed in a canoe, you don't want to dethrone the monarchy or get into the local community group who trying to preserve a oak tree at the bottom of the road what ready to fall down on top of some unfortunate black man, and want your signature, too, on the list what protesting against the Council chopping the rarse of it down and getting it over with? ('You won't sign?' the old dear ask me. 'No,' I say, 'that bloody tree like it just about to fall whenever I passing.' 'It will never fall on *you*,' she say, as if Black people immune from the vagaries of rotting trees.)

By the time Bob return from his nocturnal ramblings I had worked myself up into an evil mood, and wasn't able to add a word to my Memoirs.

'Why don't you turn in?' Bob say.

'In a while,' I say, wanting to calm myself before going to sleep.

'Is there anything you want before I go?'

14

'No,' I say, 'just wash up the tea things. And I'll have a late breakfast.'

▲ ▲ ▲ ▲

Blessed be the coming of this new generation of Black Britons, and blessed be I that I still alive and well to witness their coming of age from piccaninny to black beauty. It is a sight for sore eyes to see them flounce and bounce about the city, even if they capsize on their platforms and trip up in their maxis. Be it bevy or crocodile, Woman's Lib or Woman's Tit, they are on the march, sweeping through the streets. You see one, you see two, you see a whole batch of them. There are no women in the world who could shake their backsides like a black woman. God might give white girls nice legs and high bobbies, but when it comes to backsides, Our females are in a class by themselves. It may be that they inherit that proud and defiant part of the anatomy from toting and balancing loads on their heads from the days of slavery. But howsoever it come into being, it is good to look at. Like how you see an ordinary girl tits jump up and down if she is running, thus a black backside merely pedestrianizing. And it is not only up and down, but sideways, and gyrating in circles, and quivering and shivering in all manner of movement. It is not their coming to look at, but their going. It is after they pass you and you turn your head and look that you realize what a great experience you are experiencing. White window cleaners and navvies digging up the road want to drop everything and follow the pied pipers. Men no longer contemplate blonde and brunette and redhead, but seek the delights of brownskin, octoroon and ebony. Instead of the pale pink landscape to the foot of Mount Venus it is a dark and dusky journey filled with unexpected pleasures. The tide is turning, yes sir. Men are casting an appreciative eye on the dusky damsels floating about in town. In fact, some white men are taking the initiative and snatching up black things before the black man has a chance. Whereas it used to be the top of the social ladder to be seen escorting a white piece in the Dilly or the Circus, brothers are scorning that sort of thing nowadays, and as these black beauties grace the scene, it is to be noted that they are fecundated soon enough. Of course, the

15

English people are very happy about this competition against the white girls. Not that the new strain tries very hard; they are fully aware that before they cropped up white pussy was all the rage, and they give the brothers a hard time.

I was admiring a bevy of them as they come trouncing in the market in Shepherd's Bush one morning. They make for one of those shops what does sell everything for the head except brains. Iron comb to straighten your hair, pomades and lotions to make it shine, and of course, wigs. Wigs is in now. All kinds of Afro hair styles on display in the shop window, mixed up with some blondy, long-haired ones for those who have aspirations to be fair.

The girls stand up by the window looking in like professional head hunters, then they went in and start to try on wigs. I don't know if you have seen them women in C & A or Woolworths trying on hats, how they turn and twist and do Yoga exercises in an attempt to change their physiognomies to suit the hat they fancy. Also, the fashion being fairly new, they had to experiment and pit their wits against this latest female accoutrement.

The trouble with a wig, as I see it, is not that you trying on a new suite or a pair of shoes. It is actually going to be a part of you, like a new hand or nose or something. A time will doubtless come when you could buy a complete new face, or fit a different upper lip, or purchase a pair of new ears over the counter and put them on right away. But the greatest invention will be when you can walk in black as midnight and emerge as pure and white as the driven snow.

All the girls look different when they put on their wigs, standing up in front a big mirror and turning this way and that as the white salesgirl fuss over them. One try on a blonde wig for kicks and they all had a good laugh.

When they come out of the shop, all of them was sporting a head of Afro-hair and they wiggle their backsides as they walk off when they see me standing there.

All this is not to say that the comely Nordic damsels are relegated to the limbo of forgotten things. I mean, with them six-inch platforms they wearing, it lift the mini-skirt that much higher, and you do not have to bend down to tie up your shoelace to get a pin-t of thigh and panties. It is no wonder to me that that

16

poor Oriental in the newspapers had was to shove his hand up one of them crotch as she was getting off a train; every lusty-blooded Englishman must of wish to do the same thing some time or other.

But for me, personally, I have come to my senses and realize that black pussy is just as sweet as the white one, if not sweeter, and henceforth I shall only hit a white stroke for variety.

What made me change my mind was this little thing that Galahad send round by me to collect money for the cause. One evening Bob and me was looking at some white girls dancing on the television kicking up their legs so high we was just waiting to see them split something, when this black chick appear.

'Galahad sent me,' she say. 'I've come from the Party to explain to you what we're trying to do.'

If I did shut my eyes, I would of thought it was a nordic talking, the accent was so high. She didn't sound like some of them women what try to put on English and it don't fit them properly. She sound like the real thing, and I know without asking that she was a Black Briton. About eighteen or thereabouts, with Afro hair, Afro blouse, and Afro gleam in the eye. Any second, I thought she going to try that same intimidation trick that Galahad had, of raising the fist.

'Peace, sister,' I say quickly, to forestall any such intent. 'Have a seat.'

Maybe she didn't go through with it because she was holding a folder with papers. She sit down by the table, and Bob give a quick look to see what he could see, but she had on one of them maxi-skirts. None the less, when she cross the legs sedately the skirt tighten to show that there was pleasant terrain underneath.

'My name is Brenda,' she say. 'I do most of the paper work for the Party. Galahad said you wanted to find out more about what we do and what we stand for.'

All this time, from the moment the girl appear, Bob, as if he mesmerize, just looking at she and licking his lips. I have to tell you that Bob had this great ambition to make a stroke with a black woman, and he was always harassing me to get one for him. Now that one was on the doorstep, so to speak, he couldn't keep still. He jump up and say, 'Can I make you a cup of tea?'

She look at him for the first time. 'That's very kind of

you,' she say.

'Or maybe something stronger?' Bob was so thirsty that he was ready to jump on the girl right there and then, like a cock on a hen.

'All right,' she say. 'anything will do.'

Bob went to my cocktail cabinet and haul out a bottle of whisky.

'Not that!' I tell him. 'Use the gin.'

I should mention that though I smoke, I refrain from strong drink, and only have an occasional beer. But I had the cabinet stock up as becomes my new station. Only thing Bob drink so much that I had to teach him a lesson, and that particular bottle of whisky, I did wait until it was halfway empty, and piss and full it up again, telling him he could have that but leave the other bottles alone.

Bob pour a heavy slug of gin and top it up with some lime cordial.

'Ice?' he ask, like mine host.

'Please,' Brenda say. She was fumbling around with some papers from the folder. She take out a list with names, and next to the names have various sums of money.

'I don't think Galahad explained things properly to you,' she say. 'He is full of enthusiasm, and allows it to run away with him sometimes.'

'He did not have to explain,' I say. 'Allow me to put it to you frankly. It is money you are after, is it not?'

'Without funds we cannot survive,' she say. 'We only ask a donation you can afford.'

'Funds, donations, contribution – those are only words for money. You are as diplomatic as the English.'

'Well, cheers,' Bob say, pushing the glass in her hand.

'Cheers,' Brenda say, taking a sip. 'This is very strong.'

'We only keep the best gin here,' Bob say.

In fact it was some cheap unknown brand that Galahad knock off from somewhere and was flogging, and I empty it into a Gordon's bottle. The more you drink, the better it taste, though, according to Bob when he tested it out.

'As you know,' Brenda say, going into her spiel as if the gin crank her up, 'this is one of the areas of London with a heavy population of blacks. Things have never settled here. You and I know that not a day passes without trouble of some sort between black and white in this neighbourhood. How long are we going to be disorganized? We cannot resist and protest against the wrongs that are inflicted upon us unless we unite and reinforce the Party. And the Party has to be supported.'

'That sounds very reasonable to me,' Bob say. 'I am always encouraging Moses to take an active part in what is happening.'

'We have to rely on ourselves, or we will continue to be persecuted,' Brenda consult her papers. 'We have more than a hundred registered members. We are affiliated with several groups in other parts of the country.'

'If I were black, I'd join up tomorrow,' Bob say fervently.

'Oh, white members are welcome,' Brenda say. 'We are broad-minded. What we are after is justice and fair play for all.'

'Have you got any application forms?' Bob look around for a Biro. 'I will sign up immediately.' He move closer to Brenda, jamming up against her shoulder and bending down to look at the papers.

'You don't have to sign anything. Just come along to our meetings and give us your support.'

'Give me the venue and the time and date of the next meeting,' Bob say.

I was proud of myself at that moment, let me say, for having done such a brilliant job of converting him to the Black man's way, though mayhap he was more interested in getting under Brenda's maxi.

'We meet every other Friday at the Youth Centre in Ladbroke Grove. You know where it is?'

'Sure. Or I'll find out.'

All this time I was just looking at my man Bob and smiling. He was ready to join the army and be shipped off to Singapore tomorrow if he had to do it to make a stroke with Brenda.

'How long have you been living in England?' she ask me, changing her tactics, and swilling some more gin.

'Before you were born,' I say.

'My parents came from Jamaica,' she say. 'I was born and educated in this country, but I know where I stand. Have you ever been to any of our meetings?'

19

'Not yet,' I say.

'That's what they all say.' She wag her finger at me like a teacher. 'You must find the time. Apathy will get us nowhere.'

As she say that, she must of realized that all this talk was also getting we nowhere, that it was like trying to squeeze blood out of a stone. 'Well, I have some other things to do.' She start to put all the papers back in the folder. 'I hope you'll come to our meeting next Friday. It's better to see for yourself than for me to try and persuade you.'

'Wait!' Bob say. 'We can't let you go like that.' He turn to me. Come on Moses, give a donation.'

'I will think about it,' I say.

'We don't force anyone to join our ranks,' Brenda say.

'Here.' Bob push his hand in his pocket and start feeling about inside, as if his fingers have eyes and would know what denomination of decimal currency to produce. I thought he was going to come out with a fifty pee for the most, but he haul out a whole pound.

'I believe in justice for all,' he say solemnly, 'and let me say that you are one of the most beautiful girls I have ever met.'

'Thank you,' Brenda say, whether for the pound or the compliment is a toss-up.

'You not giving him a receipt?' I Ask.

'Certainly, if he wants one.' She open the folder.

'What nonsense!' Bob exclaim, as if he give away pound notes every day. 'Don't listen to Moses. He doesn't trust a soul.'

'I should give you one, though,' she say.

'Don't bother. Finish your drink, and have another,' Bob say.

Brenda give Bob a little smile, and he start to have high dreams. I could imagine him magnifying that smile into a laugh, and the laugh into a giggle, and the giggle changing to a sigh, and the sigh changing to a mild protest, and then – action stations!

He was full of action all right. He full up Brenda glass again, and dash out to the fridge in the kitchen for more ice.

'I really should be moving on,' Brenda say making no move to go on. 'I've work to do.'

'Forget the work,' Bob say. 'Relax and let us get to know you better.' He pick up the folder and toss it among his comic books. 'Would you like to look at television? Or maybe some music?'

He switch back on the television, and put a Sparrow record on the record player at the same time. 'You want a cup of coffee? You want to use the Ladies? It's just through that door.' He start to look around the penthouse to see what he could suggest again, and I wouldn't of been surprised to hear him tell she she could take the table and the mahogany furniture or anything else she wanted when she was going, having delivered, of course.

Well, though I did not have intentions originally myself, all this franticness and hither-and-thithering get me to start thinking about how I hadn't raised a black pussy since I was in England, being that the white ones were more available and desirable. Mark you, I would never of dreamed of it if Brenda wasn't sitting down right here in my yard. It may have been that subconsciously the image of that new crop of children dancing in the city had a hand in it. But all the same, I was not at a stage of thirst like Bob, and I didn't want to call him to heel nor pull my rank at the moment, thinking that the more leeway I gave him, the more liable, and pliable, Miss Brenda would be as the night wore on.

And he was restless. The television going, the radio-player playing, the drinks pouring, and my boy only bobbing and weaving, sitting down one moment and jumping up the next, standing one moment and then walking around the room, ending up by Brenda and jamming up close with his thighs against her shoulder.

'I can't look at television and listen to the music at the same time,' Brenda magnify the smile in truth into a laugh now.

'Which one would you like?' Bob stand poised to leap and switch off one or t'other. Either way he was anticipating kicks. If she want the TV, he could get she to sit on the sofa, dim the lights, and start a feel-up. If she wanted the Sparrow record, he could ask she to dance and start a rub-up. Is not often men have it so good.

'What do you want, Moses?' she ask me.

'Suit yourselves,' I say, playing it cool, watching how the scene would develop, and only thinking if I would include the episode in my Memoirs. I was still on my first can of beer but the both of them was knocking back gin like it flowing from a tap.

'I'd like to listen to that calypso record.' Brenda say.

Bob instantly switch off the TV. You know how those genii

does appear in Arabian Nights and say I hear and obey and flash about performing various jobs? Well, is so Brenda had my boy that evening.

Now, I know, though Bob don't know that I know, that white men feel they only have to wag their fingers and a black woman would a-running and spread sheself wide any time, any place, any old how, and deliver the goodies. And I could see that he was puzzled that so far Brenda was not conforming to the routine, though there were signs that *something* might come of the evening's caper. But Bob was getting impatient. Maybe he thought all this preliminary was unnecessary (though it wasn't costing him nil, except if you count the pound he did give for the cause). Whenever Brenda wasn't looking, he giving me a desperate and baffled glance, as much as if to say, 'What holding up the works, Moses?'

'You wouldn't like to powder your nose or anything?' he ask Brenda.

'I guess so.' She get up. 'It's through there, is it?'

'I'll show you,' Bob say, starting to lead the way, 'just down the passage, on your left.'

As she leave the room I call Bob back. 'Come back here Bob,' I say, 'and leave the girl to piss in peace. And the toilet is on the right, and the bedroom on the left.'

'You don't think she's ready?' Being from the North, maybe he thought it was a mare in foal, or something. These whites, North, South, East or West, have this thing inherent in them – that a bit of the you-know-what-old-boy would have them dancing to your tune. 'All that gin,' he continue to say. 'I don't understand, Moses.'

'Let Fate take its course,' I say.

Bob take a swig of drink. 'What's the delay, man? She fancies me. Let's have some action.'

'Don't rush the situation,' I say.

Bob begin to sulk. 'If you don't want to knock it, give me a chance. When she returns leave us alone.'

He charge up his glass again. The Sparrow record finish and he put on the other side.

'It looks like she's having a crap.' he grumble.

'I hope not,' I say. I hoped not because it didn't have soft toilet

22

paper, only the hard shiny kind that you get in the public convenience which I kept there for Bob, having a soft roll hidden away for myself.

Brenda come back. I do not know what was going on in Bob mind, but from the moment she come into the room, Bob pounce on she, and the both of them start to grapple. Bob didn't have any finesse, he just grab hold of her and start to drag she to the sofa.

'Let go of me!' Brenda say. She was so taken with surprise that Bob had she on the sofa before she realize what was happening. It may have been that if she was wearing a mini he might have had better luck. As things were, the maxi was crippling his style.

Brenda say, 'Wait a minute, give me a chance to take it off.'

It look then as if my boy was in business. I even get up from the table and stand to get a better view of the proceedings.

Bob was bending down over she, and hauling down his trousers. He had on one of them fancy stripe three-quarter drawers what white men like to wear. Brenda lift up the maxi as if she going to take it off. Then suddenly Bob disappear from view.

You remember how in the old days when they taking photo how the photographer used to go under a big piece of back cloth what cover him and the camera, as if a mystery was happening to get the photo? Well Brenda had Bob wrap up in the maxi like that, and she was cuffing him. You remember the Black Power signal of the fist in the air? Well Brenda fist wasn't just hanging. It was coming down and going up like a piston. She cuff up Bob with one hand while the other keep the maxi tight around him like a straitjacket so he couldn't move.

'You beast,' she say as she cuffing him. 'Next time you want something, have the manners to ask for it. Learn to respect womanhood. I am not one of your white flossies ready to jump into bed at a moment's notice. There are ways of going about it. You think just because I am black I am easy to get.'

What I really had to admire was the way that Brenda was doing and saying all this. It wasn't as if she was panicky and struggling to get out of a rape, and beating hell out of him. She was talking in a calm voice, like a teacher scolding a naughty schoolboy, but walloping him with some hefty ones at the same time, if you see what I mean. She had method.

23

I was just waiting to see how the photo would turn out after all that.

Bob emerge from under the maxi with his nose bleeding, his eyes bound-up, his lips bust-up, and he stagger back like a drunk and fall down on the floor.

'You should teach your friend how to behave.' she tell me.

'I've tried,' I say. 'Maybe his lust ran away with him. It could happen to any man with a girl like you.'

'Look at my bloody skirt,' she say, not meaning to be literal, but was. It had stains all over it.

'When men are thirsty they become evil,' I say. 'Bob is not really like that. When you get to know him he's different.'

Bob stagger up from the floor, and stand up swaying like a coconut tree on the beach in a strong wind.

'I didn't mean anything.' he say, rubbing blood off his face. 'You'd better go and clean up,' I say, 'you are bleeding bloody blood all over my carpet.'

All the steam was gone from Bob. Whereas he was like a lion, he went out like a lamb.

'Have you got anything I can take off these stains with?' Brenda ask me. She was lifting up the maxi to show me. The steam that did go from Bob was coming in me, but I know that if I didn't play it cool, I would end up in a corner playing with Miss Palmer, as Bob was probably doing now. I talk breezily. I say, 'Take it off, and let's see what we can do.'

So Brenda haul the maxi off, and stand up there in a black panties. I then knew what Galahad meant when he said black is beautiful. I only got a fleeting glimpse, because she fling the maxi like one of them Mayaro fishermen casting his net, and cover me over. Like we was really having ye olde photography night. I haul it off quick, in case she wanted to play the same trick on me and thump me a few. But she just sit down on the sofa watching me as I pour some gin on the stains.

'You sure that will work?' she ask dubiously. 'I've never heard of gin removing bloodstains.'

'Nor me,' I ay, 'but let's see. You want another drink?'

'I've had enough,' she say, holding her head and groaning.

'I must apologize for my friend,' I say, making a pretence of rubbing the stains off, and sitting down next to she and edging up

24

close. 'But I see you can take care of yourself.'

'If he did not catch me by surprise,' she say, 'you might have seen a memorable demonstration of kung-fu. I'd have had him splattered against the wall. But you just sat there and did nothing when he attacked me?'

'You didn't cry for help.'

'You thought I was enjoying it?'

'I don't know. Maybe you was. Were.'

'I can get a man any time.'

'I don't doubt.'

'And you'd better don't try anything yourself, or you'll get a dose of the same medicine.'

But all the same, as the dialogue went on, her tone of voice indicated that she was aroused, and England expects every man to do his duty. 'I wouldn't do anything without asking first,' I say.

But even as I was saying that, my hand accidentally stop brushing the maxi and start to brush her thighs, and she wasn't pushing me away, rather sitting back and shutting her eyes.

An old salt like me, what spend time with damsel, frauline, senorita, child, chick, bird, dolly, debutante and madam-moozel, was not to be carfuffled by a new breed of Briton. During the years of my sojourn in Brit'n, if memory does not fail me, I have fucked more than a hundred white women, give or take a few, and though I cannot keep pace with them Arabian oil tycoons who boast of having a fresh one out of the harem every night for forty-fifty years, I am proud of my average. (Never mind the quantity feel the width.) Blonde blue-eyed Scandinavian, fair English rose, vivacious Latin – all have come, and see, and I conquered.

I would qualify for being laid off for redundancy if I continue to describe the scene. Suffice it to say, that that night I learn a lesson. Kind and gentle R, you will know by now that I am not given to flights of the imagination, nor can I ever be accused of prejudice or discrimination. Witness how I take in poor Bob, and make him my footman, when he was destitute and had no place to go to when he land in London. I create a home for him, giving him the joys and comfort of a warm hearth in winter, and a fridge with ice and orange quash in the summer. Witness too that I did not even prevaricate when he assaulted the sister, but left the

25

matter in the hands of the gods.

So that when I say to you, that there is no business like black business, you know that I am not talking through my hat.

I will leave it at that, lest it begin to look as if I am curry-favouring for Our People. A word to the wise is sufficient, and Solomon say we must not gild the lily.

▲ ▲ ▲ ▲

One thing lead to another. I begin to think now of the advantages of having a regular woman about the house. I am not getting any younger, and cannot hustle pussy and scout the streets of London as in days of yore. I get tired walking, and many times I left Bob to his own resources in the Dilly or the Arch, and come home to sleep or work on these Memoirs. I see some chaps who are older than I still carrying on the routine, and all I can say is good luck to them. Since I acquire my property I does just like to come home and cool it. Sometimes I look at the television for a while, or have the odd beer, until I work up inspiration. After that glorious *salutatory* stroke with Brenda, I got to thinking that in for a penny, in for a pound, and that it might not be a bad idea to have she available on the spot. Strokes aside, there was several duties she could perform, helping poor Bob with all the jobs he had to do apart from going out to work. There is nothing like a woman's touch about the house. A vase of flowers here, a straightening of the bed sheet there – I don't have to elaborate.

It so happen that I – or rather Bob – had the basement free around this time, and I offer it to Brenda in return for household and other duties. She agree on condition that I did not mind her business nor she mine, and a few days later she move in, lock, stock and barrel.

Galahad was elated with this development, falsely construing it as my acquiescence to back the cause.

'There are more ways than one of serving,' he say.

'I don't know what you mean,' I tell him. 'I consider my deal with Brenda to be a good investment. I expect her to earn her keep with certain performances.'

'You have given the sister a roof,' Galahad say, 'and quarters from where she could conduct the affairs of the Party. It's a noble gesture to your true, inner feelings.'

I didn't bother to correct any misconceptions he had. In fact, I never bothered to even go in the basement, as she would come up to the penthouse if and when required, and of course I left all the household paraphernalia to she and Bob, who was back in grace and hitting one when I wasn't batting.

All this time Brenda was settling down to some serious work for the Party, unbeknownst to me. The basement stockup with all kinds of Black literature, Lamming and Salkey and Baldwin, and photos of famous Black men whatever their fields of endeavour, pin-up on the walls, and advertisements and notices of various publications and forthcoming and forthgoing meetings, parties, dances, lectures, miscellany for sale and wanted, and all that jazz. Worse yet, the clan was gathering in my basement to plot and plan the overthrow of the White Race and the Uprising of the Blacks, by fair means or foul.

It is said that tenants live in a house and do not know or see one another, but it has never been said until now that landlord live on the premises and don't have a clue what going on in his own house.

Then one Sunday morning, whilst I was sitting by my front window reading the *News of the World* before tackling the *Times* and *Observer*, and Bob was browsing with his comic books, I happen to glance out and notice a set of black people cluster up in the road, with placards and pieces of cardboard what have writing on them. The people have these things hoist up high in the air, wiggling them, and they chanting a refrain. Now I know that Our People like their little fetes and jump-up, and it occur to me that this crowd was getting in a little practice for a Carnival or some such prank. When I look good, though, I notice what written on the placards: KILL ALL WHITE PIGS, BLOOD AND SAND, TOO LATE SHALL BE THE CRY; and REMEMBER PEARL HARBOUR. It didn't look like the names of any Carnival bands to me. And listen to the chant: 'Power. What Power? Black Power.'

And in the vanguard of this mob was nobody but Miss Brenda and Sir Galahad.

Well, I buy a house, I didn't buy the street, and if nothing else I

27

am democratic about the rights of the masses to express their frustrations in demonstrations, if it so please them. But as the crowd moving down the road, I notice that the people who bringing up the rearguard emanating from my basement.

I push open the window and poke my head out. 'Brenda!' I yell, 'what the arse happening down there?'

Brenda look up to the penthouse wiggling a placard on a tall pole as if she want to *chook* me with it.

'Moses!' she scream. 'Come and join us! We are going to demonstrate in Trafalgar Square!'

And Galahad: 'Come on, Moses! Swell the ranks of the righteous!'

'What I want to know is why the arse those people coming out of my basement,' I yell.

But by this time she and Galahad was out of earshot, and some of the militants looking up at me in disgust, as much as if to say that I had the gumption to worry about trivia like a old basement when they were setting out to revolutionize the country.

But my basement was no trivia. I went downstairs to see what was going on, only to meet a tall, bearded member wearing a leather jacket and a wool cap, sitting down sorting out a pile of newspapers on the floor.

'Peace brother,' he greet me, looking up. 'You are late. The others have gone.'

'What are you doing here?' I demanded.

'If you hurry you could catch up with them,' he say.

'Did you hear my question?' I ask.

'I am clipping some newspaper reports for the sister,' he say. 'I am the landlord,' I say, mustering some dignity to put him in his place.

'That's cool,' he say. 'Sister Brenda is not here.' And he went back to his job as if dismissing me.

Well I really had to laugh. Long ago if the landlord come in my room I jump to attention and salute. It look as if I should of been saluting my boy instead.

As I look around I notice all sorts of boxes and cartons. The basement wasn't only plastered and decorated with pictures and notices, but it look like the Black Army headquarters.

'What's been going on down here?' I ask.

28

'You don't know about the demonstration?' he say.

'That doesn't interest me,' I say.

'Oh-h-h,' he say, slapping his forehead. 'You're Moses!' And he nod his head a few times, as if that explain everything. 'The Sister said to tell you nothing if you came. She said if you have any questions she will answer them herself.'

'You best hads clear out from my house,' I say. 'I don't like strangers on the premises.'

'Cool it brother,' he say. 'I hear you have some funny ideas, but we all hope you will see the light.'

'I don't want to have a rap,' I say, 'I just want you to go.'

The brother shake his head and smile tolerantly, and went on with the clippings.

Things have come to a pretty pass in Brit'n when a landlord ask a stranger to leave and the stranger laugh. It is not that he and me both black, no sir, it is these new laws in the land which give tenants more rights than landlords themselves. Can you imagine the audacity of this man, sitting down in my basement as if he own it, not only refusing to budge, but furthermore ignoring my presence?

The whole thing come as a joke. I wanted to laugh. 'Do you mind, sir,' I say sarcastically, 'if I have a look around?'

'The sister wouldn't like that,' he say. 'You'd better come back when she returns.'

Well, well, well. I was mad to go and call a policeman to throw this man out. And then I begin to think that suppose the law come and discover subversive literature, or even a cache of arms and ammunition in my house? My blood run cold.

I went back upstairs in a evil, brooding mood. It is always your own people who let you down in the end. I will not deny that I had ulterior motives for housing Brenda, but that was no reason for her to carry on Black Power activities on my premises.

I was barely back in the penthouse before the front doorbell ring and Bob went down to see who it was, and come back to say that a policeman was asking for the landlord.

'Shall I tell him that you are not here?' he say.

I don't know about you, but when you are a black man, even though you abide by the laws you are always wary of the police. It does not occur to you that there could be any casual contact, or

29

innocent, or even self-beneficial. It got angelic saints who would
be standing up talking about God and Jesus Christ in reverential
tones, and they see a policeman in the offing, and the meeting
break up, evaporate without a trace. A tale is told of Jasper, who
was a law-abiding citizen, a God-fearing man, a very paragon of
virtue, who found the police on his track. Jasper run. Jasper hide.
Jasper run and hide whenever and wherever he see a policeman,
although he could produce recommendations and letters of
credentials, testimonials of innocence and faith, bona fide
documents to show that butter wouldn't melt in his mouth.
Jasper grow haggard and lose weight – lose friends too who tried
hiding him, lose job too when he start turning up at irregular
hours. At last the policeman run him to earth sleeping on a bench
on the Embankment near Charing Cross.

'Jasper?' the policeman say.

Jasper was speechless.

'We have been trying to get you for weeks,' the policeman say.

Jasper nearly faint.

'A relation of yours has died and left you a large sum of
money,' the policeman say.

'I don't want it,' Jasper say. 'Please donate it to the Benevolent
Fund for Policeman.'

'That's very generous of you,' the policeman say.

'My pleasure,' Jasper say.

As soon as Bob tell me I start to think of all the crimes and
violations of the law that I committed, was committing, or was
contemplating committing. It does seem to a black man that
though he is as pure and white as the driven snow – if you will
pardon the expression – that it got something, somewhere,
sometime, what he do wrong, and that even if it don't exist, the
police would invent one to trap him.

I was prepared for anything as I descended the stairs and went
to see my visitor.

'You the landlord?'

'Yes.'

'You got a club here or something?'

'No.'

'Come on. A band of demonstrators started off from here this
morning.'

30

'I'm not saying anything until I see my lawyer,' I say.

He take out his notebook. He want to know name, address, next of kin, birthday, birthmark, birthplace, mother's maiden name, great grandfather's Christian name, date of arrival in Brit'n, hopeful date of departure, and et cetera, et cetera.

After I answer all these questions, the policeman as if he vex that he couldn't pin something on me immediately, and mad to bust a case in my arse for breathing.

'We are keeping an eye on this house,' he say. There have been suspicious characters coming in and going out. Watch your step.'

I went back upstairs and call a conference with my lackey.

'What sort of nefarious activities have been going on in this house?' I ask him.

'What do you mean?' Bob say.

'You know I've been leaving everything to you,' I say, 'you are my sub-landlord, but if you are not capable I will send you back to the Black Country.'

Bob was cool. He was surrounded by Spiderman, The Human Torch, Mr Fantastic and all his heroes. Maybe he had the idea that he was invincible in such company.

'When you gave me that position,' he says, 'you told me you didn't care what I did as long as you got the rent.'

'That was a manner of speaking, of course,' I tell him. 'I thought I could trust you. Now it appears that you are turning a blind eye because of a bit of black pussy.'

He laugh uneasy. 'You know me better than that.'

'When it comes to pussy even the high and the mighty bite the dust,' I say. 'Look what happen to lords and statesmen of the land who rise to the zenith, and lo, they crumble like ordinary mortals and succumb to the call of the flesh, and left old Brittania to paddle she own canoe.'

'Brenda is fighting for the cause,' Bob say stoutly, as if he is Black Citizen No. 1. 'She has to use the basement to hold meetings and conduct the affairs of the Party.'

'I see,' I say, although I didn't see at all. 'We will have to put some order in the chaos. I want you to keep a log in future.'

'A log?'

'Yes. I want a weekly report on everything what happen in my house. I want a list of all the tenants, their nationality, their

31

profession, and what criterions you use before accepting them. You will have to pull your socks up.'

'Balderdash,' Bob say.

'Yeah?' I say. 'Let us begin now, from the basement upwards. Who is occupying the ground floor?'

'Three tenants.'

'Names, occupations – one by one.'

'Flo. A woman from Barbados.'

'Occupation?'

'I believe she works in the station buffet in Waterloo.'

'Next.'

'Alfonso. From Cyprus. Electrician.'

'Next.'

'Ojo. African. Conductor.'

'Africa is a big country.'

'Bangla-desh or one of them new States.'

'Go on.'

'Macpherson, Australian. I don't know what his occupation is.'

'It looks like you clutter up the house with a lot of foreigners,' I say. 'Have we no genuine English stock?'

'You're not interested in the tenants,' he sneer. 'You only want your money.'

'Don't be insubordinate. Go on.'

'Two Pakis. Faizull and Farouk.'

'Hello!' This was disturbing. 'Did you check their credentials?'

'What for?'

'Man, they might of landed in Brit'n by fishing boat!'

'They pay their rent regularly.'

'Black Power in the basement,' I muse, 'and Pakis in residence – no wonder my house is under surveillance!'

'All is well,' Bob say.

'That remains to be seen,' I retort. 'We had better go on a tour of inspection. I want to see the condition you have the house in.'

'You shouldn't disturb the tenants,' Bob object, 'especially on a Sunday.'

'Come on,' I say. 'Lead the way.'

We went out on the stairway. Bob wave his hand around. 'Everything's spick and span here,' he say.

'Sure,' I say. I knew that naturally he would make certain that the carpet hoover down, and the wallpaper not peeling off, and the paint fresh and shiny, so that when I enter and ascend the stairs, everything would look all right. But what was things like under this facade? What cracks and holes lurked under the camouflage? What was the state of my Chippendale furniture, and Wedgwood crockery, albeit third hand, with which I had furnished the rooms? How was the warp and woof of my *Axeminister* carpets, and so on, and so on. I have not told you, dear R, how Bob and me fix up the rooms, how Bob only splashing paint all over the walls, and slowing down in the corners (because I have to do a bit of stippling here, Moses, you do not know anything about decorating); how he was slapping on Woolworths wallpaper, pasting it on the floor first (I hope you going to clean up all the mess, Bob); how we went scouting in the Portobello road and in Praed street near Paddington to get secondhand furniture, nor how I had him toting armchair and dumbwaiter on his back like a safari porter (Moses, we should buy everything in bulk from one shop, and let them deliver by van. How are we going to get these things to Shepherd's Bush); nor how Bob got some of his outside mates to come in and do the plumbing and gas fixtures (you will have to pay them, Bob, seeing that you are incompetent yourself). All those are minor details with which I did not want to bore you, but now that I was checking up on the human elements, I decided to look into the conditions of my materials too.

'The stairway is okay,' I say, 'but what I'd like to do is check a tenant's room.'

The first door we chance to knock at was the Pakis. Oriental melodies and talk was going on in there, but from the moment I knock, all sounds cease, like if we throw off a switch.

I look at Bob significantly. We knock again. No answer. I try the lock; it lock.

'Now I cannot even enter my own rooms,' I say bitterly.

'Tenants have rights,' Bob say. 'They are not in arrears with the rent.'

'In my days the landlord used to come and go as he please.'

Bob was starting to get vex. 'Break down the door, then,' he say.

'That's pointless, isn't it?' I say. 'We will have to repair it.'

'I don't know what's come over you this morning.' he say gloomily, 'let's go back upstairs and give you a chance to cool off and come to your senses.'

'I want a complete dossier on these two Pakis,' I tell him, 'and further more you had better start keeping an inventory of our stock.'

'You can hire a detective,' Bob say. 'That's not my job. This is just a waste of time.' And so saying, he left me and went away.

I thought that maybe he was right about disturbing the tenants on the Sabbath, but I was worried about these two men from the East. I try to peep through the keyhole but it was block.

I rap loudly and say in my stentorian, landlord voice, 'I say, you chaps. Open up, it's your landlord.'

No answer.

I say, in a nice, friendly tone, 'Come on boys, it's only me, Moses.' No answer.

I went back upstairs in a thoughtful mood, sit down with a cold beer, light up a cigarette, and ponder the situation. You does read in the newspapers about how some tenants don't know who their landlord is, and vice versa. And you does read about how the police unearth a den of prostitutes, and the opulent, top bracket landlord disclaim all responsibility, saying, 'Good lord, I never knew my premises were being used for immoral purposes.'

Mark you, as Bob remark, as long as the rent was coming in, I shouldn't of worried. And besides that, having been victimized and harassed and hounded myself, I was not altogether unsympathetic to unfortunates in similar circumstances. But *after we is weevil*, and I had to look after my own interests. I just could not afford to have my house under suspicion of harbouring illegal immigrants and Black Power militants. If to say I was living somewhere else myself, I could pretend like them social landlords that I didn't have a clue what was going on. But living under the same roof make me guilty of conniving and condoning. Ensconced in my penthouse and enjoying my hard-earned retirement, I had allowed my affairs to get out of hand. If things continued at this rate, I would soon be on the downward path, fetching and carrying, back to the old basement room in Bayswater and pigfoot and neck-of-lamb, and what-happening

Moses.

I had a sudden feeling to get out and take the air. I did that, dressing and going out and catching a bus 88 (as the Continentals say), and I hop off in Trafalgar Square because the traffic was jam and it was as good a place as any as I had no destination. It might of been that I had it in the back of my mind that I might meet one of the old timers, see a friendly face and coast a old-talk and forget my worries. The experience of that policeman coming and knocking at my door and asking all them rarse questions had me depress. I don't know if I can describe it properly, not being a man of words, but I had a kind of sad feeling that all black people was doomed to suffer, that we would never make any headway in Brit'n. As if it always have a snag, no matter how hard we struggle or try to stay out of trouble. After spending the best years of my life in the Mother Country it was a dismal conclusion to come to, making you feel that one and one make zero. It wasn't so much depression as sheer terror really, to see your life falling to pieces like that.

I couldn't see nobody I know in that melee of blacks at the rally. All I could see is fists in the air, and all them placards waving, and two chaps holding up a real pighead, and I wonder who would be the lucky militant to get it afterwards to make a souse. Not that the pigs wasn't represented, they was there in full force, only waiting for someone to step out of line to make a grab. Everybody was facing the *plinther* of Nelson, where the rally leaders was making subversive speeches on the loudspeakers; I spy with my little eye Galahad and Brenda 'mongst them. On top of the column the one-eye sailor was looking over the Houses of Parliament, as if he didn't want to have nothing to do with these black reprobates slandering the fair country, and perhaps wondering why the arse a regiment of artillery don't just sweep across the square and wipe them off the face of Brit'n.

'Blood will run!' a rally leader was shouting. 'Black Power is here to stay. We will slaughter the pigs because there is no other remedy. Brothers and Sisters, I say blood will run!'

And the whole mass cheering and making various sounds of approval, as if they ready to make blood flow instantaneously and slaughter a few pigs as an example. In fact, the incensement was so powerful that a fracas start up right where I standing.

35

Sudden-so men was fighting. It appear that a chap was raising his fist to make the power sign, and he accidentally cuff another in front of him, who turn round and cuff him back. Pandemonium break loose in the square. You know like how you see in those cowboy films how two chaps start a fight in the saloon, and suddenly everybody fighting? Is so this thing was. I find myself in the middle of the milling and confusion. Woman was screaming, men was just thumping out left and right with kick and cuff, and a white supporter went down and *disappear*, and God alone knows what happen to *he*.

As I was scrambling to get out of the brew, I feel a heavy hand 'pon my shoulder: it was the arm of the law.

If I had had time I would of said, 'Unhand me, knave,' but instead I say, 'Let me go, man, I ain't done nothing.'

A set of blacks was being towed, propelled, and dragged across Trafalgar Square. The place like it was full up of police, as if the whole Metropolitan force was lurking in the side streets waiting for a signal. Blue lights flashing, radio-telephones going, sirens blowing. Alsatians baring their teeth for the kill, and Black Maria waiting with the doors fling wide open in welcome.

I was in *one* panic as I find myself in this doomed company.

'Galahad!' I scream, as we pass the *plinther*, 'Galahad! Tell these people I am not a brother!'

Galahad recognize me and shout, 'Moses! You are in the thick of things, too!'

'Galahad!' I scream, and now I was almost in the arms of Black Maria, 'follow me to the station! Bring bail!'

'No fear!' he shout, 'you will go down in history as one of the martyrs. Tell the pigs that we shall overcome.'

The two policemen – it was two to every one black – dump me on top of the other martyrs and slam the doors: it sound like the knell of doom for true.

I do not know about you, but it is a shuddering thought for a black man to be lock up by the police. Once you are in, it is a foregone conclusion that they will throw away the key. There was no protests from any of the passengers saying that they was innocent and shouldn't be here, nobody struggling to get out like me, nobody saying anything at all. Like we was in the hold of a slave ship. I remember them stories I used to read, how the innocent starboy get condemned to the galleys. Next thing you see him in chains, with beard on his face, wrestling with one of them big oars like what stevedores have in Barbados when they loading the ships.

Any minute now the timekeeper was going to crack a whip in the Black Maria. I wonder if I play dead if they would jettison me in the Thames as we passing, and I could make my escape.

▲ ▲ ▲ ▲

I will spare you the harrowing details of my brief martyrdom, the disgrace and ignobility and shame of finding myself in a cell. Suffice it to say that late in the evening Galahad came to see me, and I was never so happy to see somebody in my life before.

'Let us get out of here,' I say.

'Hold a key,' Galahad say, employing an antiquated Trinidad phrase meaning cool it. 'It is not as simple as that.'

'You didn't bring the bail?'

'Listen, Moses,' Galahad say earnestly, 'there is more in the mortar than the pestle. This is a big thing.'

'We will discuss it outside,' I say. 'Pay the bail and let's go.'

'You are a hero,' Galahad say. 'You are a martyr like Joan of Arc and them other fellars.'

I wasn't only exasperated. I start to see red. 'Look, man, leave all that rarse and pay the people the money and let's blow this scene.'

'We want you to go through with the whole thing,' Galahad say. 'We want you to stay here until the case comes up. We are planning a mass demonstration on the day.'

I refused to believe my ears. I actually laughed. 'Stop making joke, Galahad. This is serious.'

'You don't see what an opportunity this is?' he went on. 'Imagine what a feather it will be in our caps when the mark bust that an innocent man has been held incarcerated by the pigs! The way I see it, you are here already right? You might as well hold on for a few days right? We will get the best lawyer in town, and your name will go down in the annals of black history for the sacrifice you make.'

I was really getting vex now. 'Just get me out of here, Galahad,' I say, 'I do not want to be a hero. You have had your fun, now go and pay the bail.'

'I want to take some notes,' Galahad say, as if he didn't hear me. 'What unmentionable brutalities have you suffered so far? They beat you up? They push your head in the toilet bowl and pull the chain?'

I began to have the uneasy fear that Galahad wasn't going to get me out of jail. 'For the last time,' I say, 'are you getting me out of this place or not?'

'Take courage,' Galahad say. 'I will make friends with the turnkey and see that you get some water to drink when you thirsty. Meantime consider what a blow you will be striking for the Party.'

▲ ▲ ▲ ▲

It was not until the following morning that Bob appear on the horizon with the bail, and I was released from prison. I took a deep breath of the sweet London air, and start to cough and couldn't stop until Bob hit me on the back. Up to now I didn't say a word to him, I was so overcome with the experience.

'I came as soon as I could,' Bob say. 'You have a good case against the bastards. Galahad says the party will stand behind you and see that justice is done.'

'Fuck you, fuck Galahad, and fuck the Party,' I say bitterly. 'From now on I am a different man.'

'That doesn't sound as if you're different,' Bob say.

'Action will speak louder than words,' I tell him.

'You're going to slaughter a pig?' Bob ask.

'I will slaughter the whole herd,' I say.

Writing my Memoirs in retrospective, I cannot remember all the welter of emotions that I feel at the time of my stretch. To tell you the truth, I wasn't so much vex with the police as I was vex with myself for going to that fucking rally. I remember lying on my bunk in my cell the night and thinking that if I did keep my arse quiet and stay at home, having a cold beer and looking at the church service on TV, I would not of got myself in this shit. It just goes to show how right I was all the time to have nothing to do with the black brotherhood. And imagine how Galahad had the gumption to propose that I stay there cooling my heels to put a feather in the Party cap! You see how black man different from white man? Look how, in *Tale of Two Cities*, when that chap was in the Bastille destined for the guillotine, how his friend went and take his place! You think you will ever get a black brother to give you his place in the bus-queue, much less rescue you from the clutches of the law? I think that if Galahad did only do me that little favour, the whole course of my life would of taken a turn, and I might of been in the vanguard of our struggle for freedom. But my brush with the law only make me realize that I had no friends in the world, that I had to *peddle* my own canoe for survival.

For two days I stay up in my penthouse, not talking to anybody, only concentrating on my Memoirs. Batman Bob would tiptoe in with a cup of coffee, or empty the ashtray, and keep all callers away from my door. He maintain a vocal silence, but I do not know if it was through respect for my literary aspirations, or if he realize that the moment he utter a word I would erupt like Etna.

I lost myself in my work, knowing that if I did not keep myself occupied I would really commit some violent crime in truth.

And then, when I was in the midst of a powerful descriptive passage, Bob come to me, like the head butler taking a visiting card on a silver platter to Sir or Madam. Only it was a dirty saucer instead, and a scrap of paper was in it. Silently he put it down on the table in front of me, and withdrew slightly, waiting for orders.

I deign to look at the paper without touching it. 'I have to see you, Moses,' the note say, and it was signed Galahad.

I could not get on with my work after this irritating interruption. Before I could tell Bob to throw him out, the door burst open and Galahad come in.

'I told you to wait outside,' Bob say sternly, talking in my presence for the first time in two days.

'Shit,' Galahad say.

'All right, Bob,' I say wearily, 'You can leave us now.'

Bob went out, giving Galahad a hard look.

'What shit is that you writing,' Galahad say, sitting down.

Another point I would like to make in passing, is the lack of social graces in Galahad. Note the invasion of my castle, note the intrusive, aggressive entrance, the brash, vulgar greeting, the annexing of a seat without invitation. But note, way and above his ill manners – note, I say, the stab at my Achilles heel! I actually wince.

'State your business and go,' I say coldly.

'You should be glad to see me,' he say. 'I got some good news for you.'

'You are immigrating to Africa?'

'No. The Party has influenced them pigs to drop all charges against you.'

'What charges, pray?'

'Boy! They come up with assault and battery, affray, breach of the peace, obstruction, drunk and disorderly, and they even swearing that they find grass on some of the boys.'

'In other words, they fling the book at you?'

'They didn't fling nothing at me,' Galahad say easily. 'It's you they were after. The Party committee wanted the whole set of you to stay inside until the day of the trial, to strengthen our case, but I convince them that a man like you could be more useful on the outside.'

'You make it sound as though your Party had me lock up, not the police.'

'It's just that they play right into our hands with them unlawful arrests,' he say. 'But they underestimate us. They ain't have the faintest idea how powerful and big the Party is. Every black man in Brit'n is behind us.'

'Not every one.'

Galahad laugh. 'Modesty does not become you. I know in your heart of hearts you are longing to join our ranks. I don't blame you for playing it cool.'

Bob open the door and poke his head in.

'Coffee?' he ask.

'Two sugars,' Galahad say. 'Brown.'

'I was not addressing you,' Bob say stiffly.

'Bring him a coffee Bob,' I say. 'Let's observe a little social grace, even if it's pouring water on a duck's back.'

'As you like,' Bob shrug, and went off to perform the chore.

'Listen Moses,' Galahad say earnestly. 'I not talking to you as a Party man now, but as an old friend.'

I laughed harshly. 'I would rather you shelter behind the Party,' I say, 'at least that way I can excuse you.'

'After what happen, you got to see that things in Brit'n have changed radically for blacks. You shouldn't let this house and easy life lull you into a sense of false security. Things are heaving and boiling and it going to have a BIG explosion, and we going to come out on top. You just cannot afford to ignore what is happening before your very eyes.'

'Aye, and what is happening in my very basement,' I say meaningfully, but the subtlety escape Galahad.

'There is a rumour in town that you are a traitor, that you have turned your back on your own people.'

'You know better than that,' I say sarcastically. No use. The ploy of innuendo doesn't work with people like Galahad.

'Though the boys want to send you to Coventry, I have defended your attitude time and again. Witness how you is the onlyest one I get them to drop charges against. Why you think I chose you and not any of the other brothers?'

'You probably hope to get something from me.'

'Right! I admit it! You see how honest I am!'

'Admitting the truth isn't honesty,' I say.

'I am trying to show you that the Party don't need you, but you need the Party.'

I laugh harshly again. Men will try all kinds of chicanery and bamboozlement to trap you. Note how the argument turn vice versa: he is now trying to persuade me that it will be to my everlasting benefit to attach myself to the band wagon. He must of thought I fall off a tree!

'You don't notice how all the workers belong to a union? Why you think that is so? Because each man stand to gain when he have the whole union behind him. The bosses fire one man, and the whole staff go on strike! You understand?'

'Your peurile reasoning? Of course. That is why the country is in such a mess.'

'Don't talk like a Capitalist, man! If it wasn't for the Party, you would have all them charges hanging on your head.'

41

'Galahad,' I say. 'I will tell you one thing that I have learnt in this life. It is that the black man cannot unite. I have seen various causes taken up and dropped like hot coals. I have seen them come together and then scatter like when you pitching marbles and you hit a set of them in the *rings* and they fly off in all directions.'

'The old days, the old days,' Galahad say patiently. 'It is just as I thought. You don't know that the black man these days is a different creature. He realizes that if he doesn't co-operate and cling together, all is lost.'

'The realization is there, I grant you. It's to make it work. Who is going to be captain of the ship? Who is officer number one? Who is treasurer? Who is head and who is tail?'

'If you would only come to one of our meetings, you will see how we have all that organized.'

Bob come back with the coffee.

'What are you boys rapping about?' he ask.

'Black business,' Galahad tell him. 'You won't know about that.'

'Power to the people,' Bob say. 'But you are wasting your time Galahad, you will never get Moses to join.'

We had a coffee break, and after Bob take away the cups, Galahad change the topic and came back to the matter of my work, with the same original question.

'What shit is that you writing?'

'I am composing my Memoirs,' I say, stiffly, hoping that my tone would put him off.

You don't know one fucking thing about what's happening, Moses.'

'Memoirs are personal and intimate,' I say. 'They don't have to be topical nor deal with any social problems.'

'That's no fucking use,' Galahad say. 'Nobody ain't going to be interested in anything you have to say. If you was writing about the scene today, and the struggle, I might of got the Party to back you. In any case, who tell you you could write?'

'I am not an ignoramus like you,' I say, beginning to loose my cool.

'You think writing book is like kissing hand? You should leave that to people like Lamming and Salkey.'

'Who?'

Galahad burst out laughing. Derisively, too. 'You never heard of them?'

I know of Accles and Pollock, but not Lamming and Salkey.'

'You see what I mean? Man Moses, you are still living in the Dark Ages! You don't even know that we have created a Black Literature, that it have writers who write some powerful books what making the whole world realize our existence and our struggle.'

'So? Well, my Memoirs will create a new dimension.'

'A new diversion, you mean,' he sneer. 'You tackling something what you don't know one arse about. This is a big joke! How you expect to stay lock up in your room, and don't go and investigate and do research, and take part in what is happening, and write book?'

'Let me remind you that literary masterpieces have been written in garrets by candlelight, by men who shut themselves away from the distractions of the world.'

'That's a lot of shit!'

'You are overstaying your welcome,' I say coldly.

'I going,' Galahad say, getting up to go, 'but you *gone*, man! I now beginning to understand why you been acting this way. You heading straight for the madhouse. This derelict that you buy, and your quasi-frontage of luxury, blow your bloody brains. The next thing I know you will be talking to yourself in the streets as you head for the Arches in Charing Cross to join the tramps and drop-outs.'

'And you will have to move up to give me room', I sneer. 'Bob!'

Bob come.

'Show Galahad out,' I say.

'I was thinking all the time that you had some good reason for living like a anchorite,' Galahad say as he reach the door, 'but I can see you are going to the dogs. Now I could only have pity on you.'

'Your petty jealousy is in keeping with your character,' I tell him. 'Don't darken my doorway again.'

Galahad left me with a nasty taste in my mouth. I could withstand the slings and arrows of misfortune, but when it come

43

to my penmanship, you are treading on dangerous ground. I turn the pages of my manuscript blindly, just to feel the parchment and remind myself that there are finer things in life besides black people. It was hopeless to try and continue in my present fury. I lock up the manuscript in the bottom drawer of the sideboard, where I always keep it, and put the key in my pocket. I was in such a rage that I didn't even know when I was doing all that, I just find myself heading for the door.

'Have you finished working?' Bob ask.

'Yes,' I say, 'I am going out for a breath of fresh air. Don't forget to put a hot water bottle in my bed.'

I went out and just start to walk aimlessly down the Uxbridge road.

'That bastard,' I mutter, 'you could never get a word of encouragement from a black man when you aspire to the arts or philosophy or anything above the low level they set themselves.'

And walking along in a blind despair talking to myself, I suddenly realize I was doing the selfsame thing that Galahad divine for me.

see p43

▲ ▲ ▲ ▲

During the next week or two I keep thinking about what Galahad say. The man really upset my applecart. I have weathered many a storm in Brit'n, and men will tell you that in my own way I am as much part of the London landscape as little Eros with his bow and arrow in Piccadilly, or one-eye Nelson with his column in Trafalgar Square, not counting colour. I have been mentor and mediator, antagonist and protagonist, father and mother too, a man for all seasons and reasons. There are those who will remember that if it wasn't for me, Galahad would of catch his royal arse in Brit'n. It was me who put him on his feet, share my basement room with him, console him in his distresses and lend him twelve and a half new pence when he was broke – in those days it was two-and-six, before they decimalize the currency. I have chronicled those colourful days in another tome, and it is not my wont to hark back to what is done and finish with. But I can't help remembering how I was good to him, and for him to turn around and insult my work was a hard thing to bear. I wouldn't of minded if he did call me a black bastard, or if he refuse to serve me in the pub, or even piss on me like them pigs piss on that poor African chap up in Leeds, and cause him to jump in the river Aire and drown himself. At least, so one story goes ...

I try to put down a few words, but I couldn't write anything. I just sit down there, morose and dejected. Bob must of thought that I was going through one of those periods when the inspiration wouldn't come, that we scribes know so well, for he was very discreet and did not make a nuisance of himself. But in truth I was brooding. Suppose, just suppose, that there was an element of truth in what Galahad say? Suppose when I finish, and ready to present my Memoirs, nobody want to read them? Suppose he was right, and I should start to write about Black Power, and ESN schools, and the new breed of English what are taking over the country? And what about all them Pakis and Indians who swim across the Channel and sneak ashore, or hide in them big trucks what come from the Continent?

I could feel a stirring of my mental processes, I could feel a tickle and a tingle in my thoughts, In this selfsame house dwelt two Pakis who might provide the very impetus I so sorely needed to get back to my opus! Men of mystery and topicality, men in the news and views, for it is a well-established fact that when the communication media tired lambasting the Blacks and the Paddies, they take a lag in Paki arse. Naturally the whole structure of my work would have to be drastically altered if I was to incorporate these other aspects. I mulled, I mooned, I went into a brown study, wondering if I could kill two books with one pen, as it were. It might appear to you that I waste a lot of time hemming and hawing before going into action, but you must remember that scribes does take years to produce a book, but meantime their minds are working assiduously on plot, dialogue, continuity and other technical points. Thus, I was already seeing Messrs Faizull and Farouk as them two Indian chaps from Trinidad who kidnap that woman from the *News of the World* and create a sensation. Maybe my two boys could come up with something even bigger! Maybe they would provide enough drama and intrigue not only for a book but for TV and the films!

I dash down the stairs on a wave of inspiration, and knock at their door.

'Open up,' I say briskly. 'This is your landlord speaking.'

I was lucky this time. One of them open the door.

'Yes?' he say.

I didn't have any cut-and-dried plan in mind how to approach him. 'I just want to make sure you boys are comfortable,' I say. 'Everything all right?'

'Yes,' he say.

'I'd like to have a look around,' I say.

'Sure,' he say, and move out of the way to let me pass.

Everything look usual to me. In fact, it was reminiscent of the days when I myself had to live in cramp-up quarters like this. How the both of them manage to move around without colliding called for great navigational skill.

'You are …?' I ask.

'Faizull.'

'And Farouk?'

'Working.'

It didn't look like I was getting very far with my boy and these monosyllable replies.

'I don't know any Pakis,' I say conversationally, 'although there are a lot in the country. Have you been here long?'

'Yes.'

'You like the people?'

'Yes.'

'A lot of interesting things must happen to chaps like you,' I venture.

'Such as?'

'Well,' I say, 'let's start from the beginning. How did you arrive in Brit'n?'

'By boat.'

'Ah,' I made a mental note. 'Via the Continent?'

'What're all these quesions for? You working for the police or something?'

'Those pigs!' I say scornfully, looking around as if I want a place to spit.

'If it's anything to do with the rent,' Faizull say, 'you'll have to wait until Farouk comes back. He attends to that.'

'I am talent scouting for the BBC,' I say. 'I am looking for interesting subjects who could appear on *This Is Your Life.*'

'That's an ITV programme,' he say.

'I am a freelance,' I explain. I was forgetting that these days every manjack looks at television, like drinking a glass of water or putting on a shirt.

'You'd better see Farouk about that,' Faizull say. 'Nothing interesting ever happens to me. I just go to work, and come home to sleep and eat, like everybody else.'

'That Is Your Life?' I ask.

'Yes,' he say.

'You Pakis must have it rough just as we West Indians.' I tried again. 'Haven't you ever been addressed as a black bastard?'

'No,' he say.

'No skinhead ever bash you?'

'No,' he say. 'I live a very ordinary life. I just go to work, and come home to eat and sleep.'

'All the same,' I persist, 'you must hold certain views about the present conditions in Brit'n. What do you think of Black Power, for instance? Are you affiliated with any party?'

'I don't know why you're asking me all these questions,' Faizull say. 'I can't help you. I just go to work, and come home.'

I was getting desperate. 'Maybe you know of somebody who might qualify for a programme,' I say. 'You have no friends down in Southall?'

'Look,' he say, 'Farouk might be able to help you. Do you want me to send him to see you when he returns?'

I could feel all my inspiration draining away like perspiration. This was proving to be a very dissatisfactory interview. I wonder how them other writers does find out things from people if all of them noncommittal as my boy? How the arse I was to make my Memoirs topical and gripping if chaps won't loosen up and spill the beans? I could imagine that Master Farouk might turn out to be even more taciturn than Faizull.

'What sort of guy is Farouk?' I ask. 'Is his life as interesting as yours?'

'He will be back later,' Faizull say. 'You can ask him yourself.'

I decided to make one last effort. 'Boy,' I say warmly, 'if I tell you about the things that happen to me in this country! White man spit on me, they lock me up in jail and throw away the key, they refuse to give me any work. I have some harrowing and terrifying experiences. How about you?'

'You are the one who should go on *This Is Your Life*,' he say.

I went back upstairs and open a can of beer. I wasn't beaten, I was only taking a break, planning various avenues of research, and plotting some strategy and stratagems of how to go about this new enterprise.

A few days later, I was seated near the rear window which overlook the back of the house, mulling over a fresh chapter, when I hear a bleat.

Now, you don't hear a bleat in London. You hear traffics, and all the other various sounds of milling humanity, but you don't hear a bleat, nor a moo, nor a neigh, or even a bark, as the dogs is so well-trained. So when I hear this bleat, I really didn't believe. But I hear it again.

Bob was sitting across the room looking at a Spiderman comic.

'Bob,' I say, 'do you hear anything?'

'Like what?' he ask.

'Come over here,' I say, 'and listen.'

Bob come and both of we listen. We hear it again.

'It sounds like a moo,' Bob say.

'Oh no. It's a bleat,' I say.

'Well, an animal of some sort,' he compromise. 'But I have never heard a bleat in London.'

'Nor me,' I say.

Bob lean against the glasspane and look down into the backyard.

'Hello!' he say. 'There's something down there in the bush.'

I look. I have not described the backyard before because it really shame me. It is like a junkyard and a piece of jungle in one. It is a dumping ground for old rusty bedspring and break-up furniture and old cookers and a miscellany of other jetsam and flotsam, not only from present occupants but what left from the previous tenants. I try to get Bob to clean it up once, and hire a skip to take it away, but he never got around to it. That's the junkyard part I just tell you about. The jungle part, well, a miscellaneous wild variety of flora and fauna was running riot behind there: if I had Tarzan as a tenant it would of been ideal for him.

What Bob saw, and what I see, was a sheep munching at some scrubby grass that manage to defy the environment and thrive. It was tethered to a rusty car door, and it did finish the grass nearby and was straining to reach further, that's why it was bleating.

The sight was unusual, to put it mildly.

'What that sheep doing down there, Bob?' I ask.

'Search me,' he say. 'Do you think it escaped from the zoo?'

'And found its way to Shepherd's Bush, eh?' I say facetiously, but the witticism was lost on Bob.

Now, I know it had a chap in the market what keep live chickens in coops, and you pick which one you want to buy and he slaughter it on the spot for you. But I didn't know nothing about sheeps. Sheeps wasn't in my scheme of things at all, and it present a conundrum.

As we was speculating, we see Faizull come out with a pan of water and put it down near the sheep.

'You want me to find out what's going on?' Bob ask anxiously, probably remembering how I had told him to keep on his toes.

I wasn't sure. I was adding two and two together rapidly in my mind and making five. The sight of Faizull minding sheep in my backyard was very intriguing. I feel as if I was on the track of something pertinent at last, because, just the day before, I did read in the newspapers about some Pakis in the Black Country slaughtering animals in their back gardens, and how the English people rise in arms against this barbaric custom.

So what I tell Bob is no, I decide to play it cool, and see what Faizull was up to.

The next evening me and Bob spy again, and see the sheep still there.

'I think Faizull is starving the poor animal,' Bob say.

'It ain't have much to feed on down there,' I admit.

'Couldn't he give it some Kit-E-Kat or some Lassie?' Bob was really getting anxious about the situation: you know what English people are like when it comes to animals. I used to wish I was a dog when I first come to Brit'n. 'Aren't you going to do anything about it, Moses?' he went on.

'Cool it,' I say. 'I want to see how this develops.'

'You ought to report him to the RSPCA,' Bob say. 'If you don't, I will. How can they keep a lamb? We are not a farm. I could understand if it were a dog or a cat. And even so, I don't allow the tenants to keep pets.'

Faizull come out with a pan of water, and while the sheep was drinking he was feeling it all over as if he wanted to see how fat it was getting.

'Why is he doing that?' Bob ask.

I didn't want to voice my suspicions lest Bob fly off the handle.

'I think I'll have a word with him,' I say.

I went downstairs and went outside and joined Faizull. When he see me he look startled.

'That's a nice sheep,' I say, wanting to put him at ease, lest he get the wind up and spoil the chapter I was anticipating.

'Yes.'

'Where did you find it?'

'On a farm.'

'You don't see people keeping sheep in London.'

'It belongs to Farouk.'

'You should have a proper pen.'

'I know you have rules about not keeping pets. But we'll get rid of it over the weekend.'

'You're going to sell it?'

'No.'

'Give it away?'

'No. Listen Moses,' he say, 'you don't have any objections if we slaughter it out here?'

'Good gracious,' I say, 'you mean kill it? Why?'

'It's a religious feast-day on Sunday,' he explain.

'Couldn't you get a leg o' mutton from the butcher's?'

Faizull shake his head. 'We don't eat English meat. This has to be specially slaughtered. There are certain rites to be observed.'

'I see, I see,' I say, but at the same time look regretful. 'I'm afraid it's out of the question.'

'If you allow me to do it, you can see for yourself on Sunday morning.'

He was playing right into my hands, but I didn't want to appear too willing unless I could get him to talk more freely and make my research easy.

I frown. 'This is very unusual. What will the neighbours say?'

'You can have the neck,' he say.

50

I laugh. 'There was a time when I might of been grateful for that, but I only eat chump chops or fillet now.'

'All right,' he say grudgingly.

'I haven't agreed to the killing yet.'

'I am giving you the choice cuts.'

'What I really want is your views on current affairs. How does the Pakistan community react to Black Power? What trials and tribulations do they have to overcome? What about that story I read about, how chaps who ride motor-bikes got to take off their turbans and wear crash helmets?'

'That's the Sikhs.'

'Well, whatever you call them.' I wave it aside. I wasn't going to divide up the Asian races, research or no research. Besides, I know that English people so stupid that the whole lot of Orientals and Blacks is the same kettle of fish as far as they are concerned.

'I told you already,' Faizull say. 'Farouk is the one who can help you with all those answers.'

'I haven't been able to clap eyes on him.'

'I gave him the message. I will tell him again to come and see you.'

I went back upstairs, full of eastern promise.

'Did you reprimand him?' Bob ask.

'He's going to get shot of it,' I say.

'It's a good thing.' He seem relieved. 'I had a pet once.'

'A little lamb?'

'No. It was a joble.'

'Never heard of it.'

'It's like a big rat,' he explain.

'When I was small,' I tell him, 'we used to catch rats and take it to the Sanitary Inspector in the town hall, and get a few pence for it.'

I couldn't wait for Sunday to come, so I could observe the whole ceremony and take notes. I wish I did have a camera, to take out some photos, just to reinforce the chapter I was hoping to write. Meantime, I wait for Master Farouk to visit me, but he didn't turn up. I went to the room, but neither he nor Faizull was there. The Saturday, I went into a Indian shop in the market, as part of my research. As how yam and saltfish become part of the

51

English scene with the coming of the blacks, so hundreds of little Indian shops have opened up all over the metropolis, and the Englishman no longer has to risk a perilous voyage to obtain the spices of the East; they are right here in the high street.

Sometimes in these shops you come across an Englisher who spend a day in India and feel he know all about massala and papadum. You could always tell the type – he have a shopping bag to hide the things he buy, lest he meet a friend and have to explain the quaint items. And he examining everything in the shop, even making bold to sniff the curry powder or feel the mangoes to see which one ripe, as he observe the natives do in India. And he eager to show off his knowledge, you see.

'Have you got tandoori paste and basmati rice?'

'Have you got ghee and iglee and fresh coriander?'

'Do you stock vindaloo and chapatee and basan flour?'

Like if he want to show he know more about Indian food than the shopkeeper himself. And he would start to sing the song of India, about the Taj Mahal, and the Ganges, and how he went to the palace of a Maharaja and how he cross the North-West Frontier, and want to know if the shopkeeper come from Madras or Calcutta. To all of which the shopkeeper with that servile manner which Clive of India bestow on him, would rub his hand and beam and say yes and no and sometimes *acha* for authenticity, and follow the white man about the shop as he make his various purchases. And as he go out of the shop, you could see him peep up and down the road to make sure none of his acquaintances spot him load up with all these oriental products.

I head for the butchery at the bottom of the shop, that had a sign saying HALAL MEAT. A Jamaican customer was in front of me.

'You got any pork?' he ask the butcher.

Consternation. It was as if a chap knock on the door of Buckingham Palace and ask if he could go inside to pee.

'Pork!' the butcher say, horrified.

'Yes, pork,' JA say.

'You don't see the sign? We only sell Halal meat here.' And when the Jamaican gone, you could see as if he want to spray the shop to get rid of the contaminated word.

I decided to stoke the fire. 'Nothing like a bit of pork' though, with some nice crispy crackling.'

'You too!' the butcher wave his chopper at me like he want to cleft my head. 'Don't you see the notice?'

'Okay,' I say. 'Give me a pound.'

'Of what?'

'Halal meat.'

'All is Halal meat.' He wave his hands at the various cuts of mutton and beef and chicken. It had a lot of meat there, and it all cut up different than you would get at an English butcher. Or if not, by the time you get it it will be, for these Indians does cut up everything to make curry. If you ask for a leg of mutton, he hardly finish weighing it before he got it on the chopping block cutting it up in little pieces. I notice that some of them English butchers have the same habit too: from the time they see that you are black, they start mutiliating your leg of pork or joint of beef without so much as a by-your-leave.

I decided to play ignorant. 'Oh, I thought Halal meat was something else.'

'Are you a Mohammedan?' he ask.

'Not exactly,' I say.

'I have no time to explain,' he say. 'Make up your mind.'

'To tell you the truth,' I say, 'I was really after a nice piece of pork.'

He turn his back on me, and start to eviscerate a chicken. When I was coming back home I meet Faizull in the road.

'What happen to Farouk?' I ask.

'Didn't he come to see you?' Faizull say.

'No.'

'I told him it was important.'

We went into the house together. 'I'll see if he's there now,' Faizull open his door and look inside and shake his head. 'He's out.'

'It's been weeks since I told you,' I say. 'I'm beginning to wonder if he exists?'

Faizull laughed uneasily. 'Whatever time he returns, I'll tell him to come.'

'Okay. Everything set for tomorrow?'

'Yes.'

'What time do you plan the execution?'

'Daybreak.'

'You mean in the morning?'

'Daybreak. Dawn. Just before sunrise.'

'You never see the sun rise in London,' I say.

'It's the propitious time,' Faizull say.

I set my alarm to go off at five oclock, wondering if I would be lucky to see the sun; sometimes you don't see it for a whole year in this country. I was restless, thinking about all the material I had to gather, and find it hard to fall asleep. I start to count sheep and by the time I reach the one in the backyard the alarm went.

Usually I had Bob bring me a cup of tea on awakening, but I did not want to incorporate him, though I thought it would be kicks to see him grow pale when blood start to spill.

It might of been a good idea to get an English aspect of the proceedings, too, but I felt he might become excited and overwrought and create a disturbance.

I went downstairs and met Faizull and another chap.

'Ah,' I say, 'this is Farouk?'

'Well,' Faizull say, 'that is his name. We have no time to talk.'

'When will we have a chat?' I ask this Farouk.

'What for?' he say. 'I am a very busy man. My services are in great demand.'

'Let's go,' Faizull say.

We went out into the yard with all the necessary paraphernalia, tripping over all kinds of rusty junk and battling through the undergrowth. Now and then Farouk, in the lead with his butcher's knife, would slash at a branch or a bramble or a liana that impeded our progress. I put my foot in a set of stinging nettles that sting me even through my trousers.

At last, panting and exhausted, we reach the small clearing. The sheep was laying down, but the eyes was open watching we.

'Try and keep out of the way,' Faizull tell me.

'I want to see every single thing,' I say, looking around for a place to rest my notebook so I could write in it. I had was to buy one to take notes in my research, but how them reporters does just hold it in their hands and write? In the end I had to pick up a piece of rotting hardboard and prop it at the back of the notebook: I made a mental note to purchase one of them square

54

pieces of wood what have a big spring clip at the top, like what you see those chaps have when voting time come and they come to survey you.

Whilst I was getting poised, Messrs Farouk and Faizull was getting ready for the dark deed. Farouk was kneeling down, facing the pearly light of dawn in the East, and with the weapon in his hands as if he proffering it to the sun to make the *coop de grace*. Faizull was tying the sheep foots together, two in front and two behind. Farouk start up a oriental chant in one of them strange tongues, Urdu or Punjabi or something.

'What is he saying?' I ask Faizull.

'Shh,' he say. 'It is a prayer. Try not to make noise. If the sheep becomes excited and nervous, the muscles will get tense and stiff, and the meat will be tough.'

'It's the sheep that should be praying,' I say.

Then, without further ago, Farouk swivel round on his knees, and before you could say Jack Robinson he lift up the sheep head and administer the death stroke in one clean movement, slitting the throat from ear to ear. It seem to me that he could of gone down an inch more from the head, but that might of meant one inch less neck to share out. Faizull jam up the plastic bucket under the gash to collect the blood, and he straddle the sheep with his hands and foot to still the death throes.

A solitary shriek of horror rent the atmosphere. It was so unexpected and piercing that Faizull lose his grip and slip off the sheep, and Farouk brandish the butcher knife and looking to see where it come from.

I was the onlyest one to keep my cool: I look up to the penthouse and see Bob leaning out of the window as if he vomiting.

'I will get the RSPCA to arrest you!' He shout. 'You too, Moses!'

Everything was going nice and smooth until this white man run amok: that's why I didn't want him in the first place.

'Shut up,' I shout. 'Another word from you and I will have *you* arrested for disturbing the peace. Shut that window, Bob, this very instant!'

I put a lot of sternness and authority in my voice, for I did not want any further noise to waken the whole neighbourhood. Bob slam down the window, but he stay behind the glass watching.

'Will he cause trouble?' Faizull ask.

'I can take care of Bob,' I say. 'Proceed.'

Farouk stick the knife in his belt like a pirate. He and Faizull haul the sheep to one of the smaller trees. They tie up the sheep foot one by one, then they spreadeagle it up on a branch upsided down with the head still hanging by a piece of skin, and Faizull put the plastic bucket to catch the blood. Then Farouk take off the head and wrap it up, like that Greek hero do with a woman head, I forget the whole story at the moment, but you know the one I mean, about the chap who had wings on his foot, and he slash off this woman head: she was so ugly he had was to look in a mirror to do it, else she turn him into stone – you remember? Farouk say that the head is a great delicacy, especially the eyes, and that he want it for himself. He say that every time he kill a sheep, he claim the head as a sort of trophy. It appear he was some sort of official slaughterer, and I wanted to ask him some questions, but he was busy now skinning and dissecting the carcase.

I never see the knife so sharp in my life. As if it only whispering, as if it just making some light, gossamer strokes and the blade flashing in and out of the sheep anatomy.

'I think I'll have some liver too,' I tell Faizull.

'We did not bargain for that,' he say. 'You should keep to your word.'

'I may have some trouble with the police over this business,' I point out.

'No,' he say, 'we have not broken the law.' And he went on to explain the legal angles.

By and by Farouk was down to the finishing touches.

'What about the golden fleece?' I ask, imagining that in due course it would make a handsome rug for me to put my foot down on when I get out of bed.

'We will have to leave it out here to dry out,' Faizull say. I wasn't sure that was safe, remembering again some other Greek and a gang of argonauts who went and thief a fleece from some king garden – you know the one I mean.

'It's all finished now,' Faizull say. 'There's nothing more to see. You can take a piece of liver now I'll bring you the rest later.'

56

'Is that all?' I was disappointed. 'What about all them rites and rituals?'

'Farouk has another job this morning,' Faizull say. 'We can't go through all that rigmarole.'

So I went back upstairs to face the melodrama. Sure enough, Bob waiting for me. Tears wasn't streaming down his face, but he certainly look distraught and woebegone.

'How could you, how could you?' he greet me.

'Have you made coffee?' I ask.

'I could try and understand those Pakis,' he say, 'but you took a hand in the proceedings. You are just as guilty as they are. Do you realize what you have been a party to? This is a civilized country, we don't do things that way. If they want to kill a sheep, they should go to a proper slaughter-house.'

'They haven't broken the law,' I say. 'It's for their own use, they are not selling it, and they are going to clean up and don't cause a hazard to public health.'

'I see,' Bob say, tight-lipped. 'You have even acquainted yourself with the by-laws, conniving with the Pakis. But what will the neighbours think?'

'Even if they peep over the wall they can't see anything in that dense foliage,' I say. 'Here.' I show him the liver. 'When last have you had a piece of fresh liver for breakfast? Feel it, it's still warm.'

Bob look as if he want to throw up.

'It's good for you,' I say. 'It will make your cock stand up.'

He begin to look interested now. 'Yeah?' he say.

'It's packed with vitamin E,' I say. 'Look,' And I squeeze the liver and let a few drops drop.

'Don't be filthy,' he say. 'You're messing up the table and I will have to clean it.'

'Season it with a little salt,' I instructed, 'and fresh black pepper from the mill. Sauté it gently in butter. As soon as the blood starts to ooze it's finished.'

'I'm not sure I can eat breakfast after what I've just seen,' he say. But you could see that the prospect of aiding the elevation of his penis had him curious. You could fool a white man with any shit if he believe it will prolong the sexual act.

He took the liver, albeit gingerly, and went into the kitchen.

Fifteen minutes later we was polishing off the liver with some onion rings that Bob fry golden. He tackled the meal with gusto, but still kept up a tirade.

'It's the principle of the thing, Moses,' he say, with his mouth full of liver. 'It's not that I'm not partial to a bit of fresh meat.'

For spite I try to put him off eating. 'Did you see how the blood spurt out of the sheep neck when Farouk make the slice?'

He stop chewing for a few seconds, but start to masticate enthusiastically again.

'That wasn't Farouk,' he say.

'How you mean it wasn't Farouk?' I ask.

'That's not the Farouk who came to see the room with Faizull.'

It was me who stop chewing now. 'Who was it, then?'

'I don't know.'

Something funny was going on here. 'When last have you seen Farouk, then?'

'Come to think of it, I haven't seen him since the first time they came looking for a room. Faizull always brings the rent. But letters come for Farouk.'

'Well, he must collect them?'

'I never saw him. But the letters are always taken away.'

After breakfast, while Bob was washing up in the kitchen, Faizull come up with my share.

'Where's Farouk?' I demand.

'He's gone.'

'When is he coming back?'

'I don't know. He lives in Southall.'

'Oh, I see. So he isn't Farouk, the one who shares the room with you?'

'Oh!' Faizull smile for the first time since I know him. 'Did you think he was my friend Farouk?'

'Yeah,' I say.

'I only said his name was Farouk.'

'Okay, okay.' I wasn't going to let no bloody Paki get the better of me. 'Let's start again. Where is the Farouk who resides in your room in this house?'

'He has gone to spend the day with some relatives. I told you we were celebrating a religious festival.'

'How is it, that I can never set eyes on Farouk?'

Faizull shrug. 'At the moment he is working a double shift. He comes and goes at odd hours. But I have told him several times that you want to see him. Maybe he is not interested.'

'It's funny I don't see him around at all.'

'He was here last night. What more can I do?'

Bob came in, and as I was telling him to take the meat into the kitchen, Faizull slip away, so quietly I didn't know when he left.

I make up my mind to find this Farouk by hook or by crook. I wasn't annoyed any more, I was just intrigued by the mystery.

I left a note in the hallway: 'Mr Farouk, I have been trying to get in touch with you on a matter of the greatest urgency. Come up to my flat, whatever the hour, when you get this message.'

The next morning the note wasn't there and I ask Faizull about it.

'He got your note, Mr Moses. Didn't he come to see you?'

'No.'

There was a long pause. Then Faizull say, 'I have a confession to make.'

Ah, I thought triumphantly, we are getting some place at last, 'Yes?' I try to keep the eagerness out of my tone.

'It's about Farouk.'

My hopes soared. 'Go on.'

'Farouk doesn't speak English.'

'Then how did he read my note?'

'I read it for him. Some of us are not like you and me, who have lived here for a long time and know the ropes.'

'What's this all about then?' I say sternly. 'Why are you sending him to me if we cannot converse?'

Faizull spread the palms of his hands out, as if the answer there. 'Well, you were so persistent, and I don't like to talk about another man's shortcoming. You will need an interpreter to talk with him.'

I decided to take the bull by the horns. 'I'm going to stay in your room until the elusive Farouk turns up,' I say.

Faizull put on the traditional inscrutable oriental expression. 'There is no telling when that will be.'

'Do me a favour,' I say. 'When he comes, don't tell him anything. Just nip upstairs and let me know, and I will come down.'

59

'Okay,' Faizull say.

As it turn out, I have to go out for a short time that evening, but I hurried back in case I miss him. Sure enough, as soon as I got back Bob say, 'Faizull was up here to see you a few minutes ago.'

I dash downstairs and Faizull open the door with a look of regret.

'Don't tell me,' I say, 'Farouk was here but I just missed him.'

'That's not all,' he say, 'He took away most of his things and said he would not be back for some time.'

'Ah well,' I shrug. 'Just forget it. It doesn't matter.'

'I'm sorry, Mr Moses. I did my best.' But he look elated.

'Not to worry, Faizull,' I say, and wanting to put him off his guard. 'I shan't be bothering you again.'

And I left him with that. But I was like a cat on a hot tin roof. The mystery was deepening, and the plot was thickening. Some skull-duggery was going on and I was determined to get to the bottom ot if.

My chance came a few days later when a letter arrived for Farouk, I saw it on the little table in the hallway as I came in, and I impounded it and took it up to my room. I sit down on the sofa and had a good look at it. It had a Dutch stamp on it, and the address was type out.

Once in the old days I had a au pair from Holland. That sound like a *parabox* but what I really mean is I was stroking it when she had time off from the English Mistress and Master in Hampstead. When she went back, she remembered them days of wine and roses what she spend with me, sweeter than tulips in Amsterdam, and she used to write letters, and send postcards with Dutch girls wearing them funny white hats what curl up, and them heavy clobbers on their foot.

First thought I had now – just to show you that I had no malicious intentions – was that old Farouk must of got himself a Dutch sleeper who went back to Holland, and drop him a line. I lift the letter up to the light and see if I could see inside, and I shake it in case it had money. But it was so flimsy, that was as if was only the envelope.

I had no compunctions about steaming it open for the sake of my research, and whilst I was in the midst of this operation Bob stroll in.

'What are you doing?' he ask.

I didn't answer because he could see what I was doing. I don't think he approved, but he was curious. We see some trouble to open it, being as it was one of them thin envelopes like tissue paper, and I didn't want to tear it. Inside had a small sheet of paper with some words type on it in capital letters, like when you get a telegram: FOUR ARRIVING SATURDAY SAME PLACE SAME TIME USUAL PROCEDURE.

I feel my scalp prickle with excitement, as my hair couldn't stand on end. 'Listen to this Bob,' I say, my voice trembling in a whisper, and I read it out for him. 'All my suspicions are confirmed!'

'Don't jump to conclusions,' he say. 'It could mean anything.'

'Not to me,' I say. 'We are on the verge of exposing an international racket to smuggle Pakis into Brit'n! What else could it be?'

'Maybe Farouk is in the import-export business,' Bob say.

'Yes, importing illegal immigrants!'

'I won't be too hasty if I were you,' Bob say. 'That letter could be quite innocent, and you may land yourself in trouble for tampering with someone's mail. I should seal it up and put it back and forget all about it.'

'You expect the gang to write him and give details?' I argue. 'What else could it mean than Farouk is the contact man in London, and four Pakis are due from the Continent on Saturday.'

'Don't let your imagination run away with you,' Bob say. 'You are looking at too much telly.'

But I wasn't going to let Bob put me off the scent. I keep the letter, but I left a note in the hallway to say I had it, and if master Farouk want his mail, he could come and collect it in person, and we would have a showdown.

Later that evening, whilst I was on tenterhooks, the door rap and Faizull come in. It look like he lose all his cool, very agitated.

'You have a letter for Farouk?' he ask.

'Yes,' I say, and then histrionically, 'from Amsterdam.'

'I will see that he gets it,' Faizull say. He stand up near the table, and I could see he was itching to snatch up the letter.

61

'Let him come for it himself,' I say, playing my ace.

'He told me to collect it for him. It is very important.'

'I will deliver it to the addressee and no one else,' I say.

Faizull look at me silent for a few moments. 'I thought you had given up the idea of meeting him.'

'No. I am more than ever determined to meet him vis-à-vis.'

'I see.' He went into a brown study again. 'I will make a deal with you. Give me the letter, and I will arrange a meeting.'

I ponder this. It sound good. It sound as if I might get right into the heart of things.

'How, when and where?' I ask.

Faizull pick up the letter as if the deal conclude. 'You know the Marble Arch station?.

I give him a wan smile. 'Of course.'

'Meet me there tomorrow at six, punctually, near the ticket booth. I will bring Farouk with me.'

I didn't like the way things was going, as if he giving all the orders and I have to obey, even though I had the upper hand.

'Can't you bring him here?'

'That's impossible.'

'Okay,' I say, and then to show him I mean business, 'this is the last chance I'm giving you. If he doesn't turn up,' I add darkly, 'we shall see what we shall see.'

Who you think was at Marble Arch at the stroke of six precisely next evening, with notebook and pencil poised? Who you think wait there like a poor-me-one till seven o'clock, then had was to catch the tube and come home in a fiery mood of destruction? Enough of all this fiddle-faddle, I vow, I would have a confrontation with Faizull and put my cards on the table, and something bound to pan out one way or t'other.

But Faizull wasn't at home. Instead, it had a telegram for Farouk, and I give it the same treatment as the letter. After I steam it open I read: IF LANDLORD NOSY EXTERMIN-ATE HIM.

It was time indeed for sober reflection, to weigh the pros and cons and see if I was pro or con. I am aware that so far the whole thing sound as if I making it up, as if after Galahad's caustic comments I am fabricating a cock and bull story to augment my Memoirs. You are at liberty to think what you will: for my part, it was plain as the colour of my skin what that telegram signify. It didn't sound as if Messrs Farouk and Co. was going to throw a banquet with me as the honoured guest. If the landlord fucking up a time, exterminate him. It could not of been couched in more simple terms.

In this life you always feel safe when something happen to other people and nothing happen to you, but whatever your station or race, colour or creed, your turn got to come, and mine was here, now. How would they bring about my demise? Weight me down with cement and fling me in the Thames? Knock me down with a bus 88 as I was crossing the zebra crossing? Line me up in Horse Guard Parade and make a execution? Maybe all them things was too grandiose: killing a black man easy as kissing hand, like swatting a blue-arse fly what get in the house in the summer.

Time, too, to rue the day that I first become involve with my tenants. Even if to say my Asian brothers was mixed up in a smuggling racket, why the arse should I interfere with them and stick my neck out? It was all on account of that bloody Galahad, who make me feel I was going wrong and needed topicality and subjects of interest. First he left my arse in jail; now he have me in danger of extinction for not minding my own business.

When you read other scribes, or see them television films, at this stage the hero will gird his *lions*, and after a series of breathtaking adventures, successfully overcome the forces of evil. If you think I was about to ditto, you are sadly mistaken. I was shaky like a aspen leaf; if a basin of water and towel was handy, I would of wash my hands like Pontius Pilate, and call it a day.

But what should happen as I sit there with the telegram vibrating in my twitching hands than the door open and Faizull walk in. Praise God, by then I did seal it back up, though that was cold comfort

'I was expecting a telegram,' he say without preamble. 'Is that it?'

Instead of saying 'No, it's from my aunt in Tobago' I was so frighten I blurt out, 'It just arrive this moment.'

Faizull snatch it out of my hand. 'What are you doing with it?'

'I was holding it safe for Farouk. Telegrams is important not like ordinary letters.'

'Yes,' he say, starting to open it. 'Maybe I should read it in case it's something urgent.'

'What happen this evening?' I ask quickly to distract him and postpone the inevitable. 'I was waiting in Marble Arch more than an hour.'

'There was a change in plans,' he say.

You're telling me, I thought gloomily. 'Listen Faizull,' I say, 'I have made up my mind. I couldn't care less about meeting Farouk. As far as I am concerned, he doesn't exist. Nor you for that matter.'

'It's a bit late for that now,' he say grimly. 'It's no longer a question of your wanting to meet Farouk. Farouk wants to meet you.'

My blood run cold. 'What for?'

'The answer may be in this telegram.' And before I could stop him he was reading it.

I start to *trimble*. One of the thoughts that come to my head, just to show you my state of terror, was to forsake the writing of my Memoirs. I do not have to say more. You will understand, gentle R, my utter collapse to come to such a heart-rending decision. I shut my eyes because I didn't want to see how Faizull would operate. Maybe he had a revolver with a silencer in his pocket; maybe he would just catch a hold of me and strangle me; maybe he might push me out of the penthouse window and pitch me down in the backyard where they already murder a sheep. In the jungle down there my body could lay undiscovered for weeks.

'Mr Moses.' Faizull voice sound cold. 'Are you listening?'

'No,' I say.

'May I sit down?'

I open my eyes. 'Yes, yes! You want a cup of coffee? Anything to eat? Bob isn't here but I'll attend to you myself!'

'That won't be necessary.' He sit down. 'The telegram has some bad news.'

I almost laugh. Bad news, he call it. My death warrant, more likely.

'I am going to take you into my confidence. Farouk might not like it, but I feel you might be useful to us.'

64

'You don't have to tell me nothing, Faizull,' I say rapidly. 'I don't want to know anything about nothing.'

'Are you working for the police?'

'Me? Work for the police? Ha ha.'

'I thought not. But you suspect I am an illegal immigrant?'

I burst out laughing till the tears stream down my face. 'What on earth gives you that crazy idea? Come to think of it, I was in Heathrow one day and I saw you coming through Customs, with your passport in your hand.'

'I came by private plane from Amsterdam, together with Farouk.'

I wanted to crouch up like that proverbial monkey what put his hands over his face and see nothing, hear nothing, say nothing. 'Anything you say, Faizull.'

'Listen. We have a good business going, and you can make some money if you are interested.'

'I don't want no money, I don't want anything, honestly.'

'That's a great pity, Mr Moses. I am taking it upon myself to make you this offer, because I do not like the alternative.'

Death, extermination, killing, alternative – call it what you like, it's the same thing.

'Let me hasten to add,' I hasten to add, 'I am not averse to your affairs, whatever they are. In fact, if you blow up Buckingham Palace I would turn a deaf ear, because I do not want to be alternatived.'

'Good. We need some place in London, where we can house newcomers for a few days until other arrangements are made. You see what I'm getting at?'

'No,' I say, though I had a pretty shrewd idea. 'You mean something like a deserted building in the East End?'

'Or a house like this in Shepherd's Bush.'

'Yes,' I say. 'What a shame I'm full up.'

'Chicken feed,' Faizull say. 'Get rid of them. You will make more in a week than a year with them.'

'It's a tempting preposition,' I say, making a pretence of rubbing my chin thoughtfully.

'It is more than that. It is your only salvation.'

I was trying hard to make my dialogue original, and not copy the cops and robbers, but all I could say was, 'You going to give me some time to think about it?'

'Not much,' Faizull say, getting up. 'What shall I tell Farouk?'

'One thing is liable to lead to another.' I stall. 'You only want to annex my property now, but later you might want me to go to the airstrip in the country to welcome your brothers, or go to Amsterdam or gay Paree on company business. You might even want me to alternative some poor unfortunate.' And I shuddered visibly.

'As long as you keep your nose clean, and don't snoop around like you've been doing, there is no reason why things should not be honkeydory. And don't forget, I am here, even if Farouk isn't around much.'

And with that Faizull left me to my thoughts, and I don't have to tell you what them was. First Black Army headquarters, now sanctuary for illegal birds of passage.

When you crooked you bend, as we say in Trinidad, meaning when you are in the shit you sink down deeper, and monkey smoke your pipe.

▲ ▲ ▲ ▲

There is no god but *the* god, and Mohammed is his prophet. A man must go where the winds of fortune blow him, willy-nilly, for his Destiny is writ on the stars, nor all thy tears wash out one word of it.

The first batch of Asians turn up at dead of night one night, and I had was to shift Bob into my flat to make room for them. Naturally I had to appraise him of the lay of the land, and the position we were in. He wanted to blame himself for taking Faizull and Farouk as tenants in the first instance, but there was no sense in chastising ourselves for anything. *Kay sir rah, sir rah*, as the Japanese say.

It was a motley trio that Faizull shepherd into the house. I have seen bewitched, bothered and bewildered adventurers land in Waterloo from the Caribbean with all their incongruous paraphernalia and myriad expressions of amazement and shock, but this Asian threesome beat them hands down. Their miens bore that inscrutability they so famous for, as if they see you and at the same time don't see you. They seem poor subjects for

66

integration to me: it look as if you can't penetrate them at all, they have you baffled from the start. Still, it takes all kind to make the world, and who was me to pass judgement?

'No luggage?' I ask Faizull.

'That will come later,' he say, and then, as if they was recalcitrant children. 'Just give them a cup of tea and send them to bed.'

Bob went to put the kettle on.

'How long are they staying?' I ask.

'Not long,' Faizull say. 'We have to keep them moving.'

'Listen,' I say, 'I hope they are not going to slaughter any sheep on the premises, nor stink up the house with curry.'

'They have to stay in their room and don't go out at all,' Faizull instruct. 'I will take them away in a few days.' He sit down and haul out a wad of money. 'Twenty pounds,' he say, counting it out. 'All right?'

I laugh mirthlessly. 'I risk my respectability and integrity for that? These chaps must have paid you hundreds of pounds to bring them in. You expect me to shelter them that paltry sum?'

'That's what Farouk says you're to get.'

'It isn't worth my while,' I say. 'I mad to report you to the police and finish with this whole business.'

'Each,' he say.

'What?' I say.

'Twenty pounds for each of them,' he say, counting more money.

'What about my man Bob?' I ask.

'I don't know about him. That's your responsibility.'

'He's liable to squeal if you don't treat him right. Don't forget he is English, and loyal to Queen and Country.'

'That's your baby. You know what will happen if there is any trouble.' Faizull put the money on the table and went out.

Bob come back from the kitchen. 'Where's Faizull?' he ask. 'I made a cup for him.'

'He's gone. You'd better give the guests the whole pot and let them sort it out themselves.'

'You think they can manage?' he ask dubiously.

'Come come,' I say, 'they may look a little dishevelled and

67

unkempt, but they are not children.'

Bob went down with the tea, but come back up with everything.

'They have locked and barricaded themselves in the room,' he announced. 'They won't open up.'

'Put it outside the door,' I tell him, 'they will take it when the coast is clear.'

When he come back from doing that he moan, 'I hope they do not shit and piss in my room.'

'Here is your cut,' I say to comfort him, and hand him a tenner.

'We are really in a sticky position, Moses. What are we going to do?' But all the same, he fold the tenner and pocket it unobtrusively.

'I don't know, Bob. What the arse can we do? Faizull has commandeered the house and our hands are tied.'

'We can't go on like this. We are aiding and abetting this illegal traffic, and will get in trouble with the law.'

'Which would you rather risk, the law or being alternatived?'

'That's a lot of nonsense, man. In this day and age, how can such a thing happen? I think Faizull is exploiting your gullibility. We should go straight to the police and make a clean breast.'

'Who shall bell the cat?'

'We'll go together.'

'Not me. Maybe Faizull bluffing, but I am not going to be the one to find out. In my experience, nothing is impossible, and whilst you might think of all this as a horrible nightmare, truth is stranger than fiction, and the fact of the matter is that he got us by the balls.'

'Maybe we should try and find out more about the whole set-up. We might discover a way out.'

'I don't want to find out nothing. That's how it all started.'

'Well,' Bob say, 'let's try and see Farouk. It seems he has more authority than Faizull.'

'Easier said than done,' I say.

Bob went into the bedroom to try and get some rest, leaving me to wrestle with the problem. Suddenly I hear bragadam, biff, and other extraordinary noises, and when I went to see what happening, I see one of the Asians on the landing outside. He had his sleeping mat with him, and he was just rising from the floor, having been precipitated violently from the room.

I was in a quandary. 'Speakee English?' I try.

'Fuck off,' he say, giving me a nasty look.

It was not the most auspicious phrase in the Queen's language, but it was handy and in everyday use, and at least I knew he was linguistic.

'What happen?' I ask.

'These two bastards in there are infidels,' he say. 'I refuse to stay in their company any longer. I am already contaminated and will have to be cleansed by a pundit. There is no god but *the* god, and Mohammed is his prophet.'

Whereupon he spread his sleeping mat and squat down facing East.

'But what happened?' I ask. 'You can tell me, I am one of the Faithful.'

'I told Faizull I did not want to mix with the others ever since we were in Amsterdam. He said it would be extremely difficult, and that he could not do anything until we arrived in England, and that it would cost me extra. I agreed and gave him twenty pounds more. Now we are in England, and I should not have to suffer the presence and proximity of disbelievers. You pays your money and you takes your choice. Have you got any Dettol?'

I went to look for Faizull, but he wasn't in the house. I come back and try the door, but it was lock. I bang, but nobody won't answer.

'You chaps have got to settle your differences,' I told Paki, 'You're not in Pakistan any more.'

'I am not spending another minute in that room,' Paki say.

'You can't sleep on the landing,' I say.

'Since I left the bonny banks of the Ganges,' Paki say, 'I have slept in all manner of places. Besides, I do not need any sleep. I might just go into a trance and catch up with my meditation.'

And so saying, Paki take up the lotus position and lose himself from worldly care and woe; he didn't even know when I left.

It's a good trick, that. Imagine when things grim and you are catching your arse, all you have to do is cross your legs and sit down, and look for the middle of your forehead, and all your worries are over.

The next morning he was still there, in the same position. I don't know how he didn't catch cramp.

▲ ▲ ▲ ▲

And not only next morning he was still there, but Paki take up
residence in the house, living in Faizull room. It seem that Faizull
needed a man on the spot to organize the traffic, and he and Paki
come to some sort of agreement. All this time I never see Mister
Farouk once, and when I ask Faizull, he say that he was in
Amsterdam handling operations from that end.

In the space of a month, twelve orientals came to Shepherd's
Bush and thank God, fold their tents like the Arabs and as
silently steal away. I never knew where they went, or what
happen to them after they leave the house. Twelve times twenty
is two hundred and forty pounds, and even when you discount
Bob's cut, you can see that I was laughing all the way to the bank.

But it must not be imagined that I accept this blood money
without trepidation and qualms. Although the other tenants
appear to be minding their own business, all this nocturnal
activity was arousing suspicion, and any day I expected the police
to make a raid. I plan I would pretend ignorant and say that I
don't know nothing, or tell them I holding a meeting of orientals
to indoctrinate them into our way of life. But I know that I was
helplessly and hopelessly entangled and ensnared, and that
monkey would smoke my pipe if the law get wind of what was
happening.

Them was perilous days, days of walking tip-toe, days of
jumping up out of bed in a nightmare, days of living dangerously
and starting at shadows. One night I dream I was in a Persian
market surrounded by millions of the Faithful and the unfaithful,
and I was asking each one if he was Farouk, and they all smiling
and shaking their heads. Then Faizull appear in the dream in one
of them big removal vans, and the whole horde start to fight to
scramble in, and I was helping to push them, and counting in my
mind forty times twenty, forty-one times twenty, fifty times
twenty. The van didn't have space for me in the end and I had to
sit down on the bonnet, but fifty times twenty make a thousand
pounds, and I was now in the four-figure bracket. And then I
start to get cold sweat wondering how we going to house fifty of

70

them in Shepherd's Bush.

I wake up from the dream in this cold sweat, and lo, there was a soft rap at the door, and when I went it was Faizull.

'Man,' I tell him, 'I just had a terrible nightmare.'

'Never mind,' he say, 'there will be no more sleep for you tonight. I have a bunch of tulips from Amsterdam.'

Faizull appear as if he too, had a nightmare, for he was sweating enough to water the tulips.

'You had a rough crossing?' I ask.

He went to the window and shift the curtains and peep out before he answer.

'After this trip, Farouk going to give Shepherd's Bush a rest,' he say.

'You mean you are releasing me from bondage?' I ask joyfully.

'Things are getting hot,' he say. 'We will have to operate in another district.'

I start to hum a little ditty. I was wide awake now, almost ready to take pleasure in my work.

'Wake your friend Bob,' Faizull say, 'while I bring them in.' I rouse Bob.

'Action stations,' I tell him gleefully.

Bob grumble and rub his eyes. 'Do I detect a note of joy in your voice?' he ask.

'Aye,' I say, 'you do. This is going to be the last train to San Fernando.'

The news perk him up too. In a little while he had the kettle on and was lining up cups.

'How many?' he ask cheerfully.

'I don't know yet,' I say, rubbing my hands contentedly. 'But this is the last time, Bob. Happy days are here again.'

'Moses,' Bob say solemnly. 'don't ever get yourself in such a situation again. I have lost weight worrying about it. The tenants have been asking embarrassing questions. And more than once I have seen policemen loitering about the corner.'

'It will all be over soon,' I say, 'and we shall revert to our former way of life.'

'I hope so,' Bob say. 'Peace of mind is better than all the money in the world.'

'I agree,' I say, 'you know that my hand was forced into this affair. When we get rid of this last batch, we shall fumigate the house and wash our hands of the whole business.'

Faizull shepherd in the refugees, and I begin to count as they come in. Twenty pounds, forty pounds, sixty, two hundred and forty.

A cold shiver run up and down my spine.

'Faizull,' I say, with a tremor in my voice. 'how many are there?'

'That's the lot,' he say.

I laugh hollowly. 'I count twelve. Even if I had a mansions, I wouldn't have place to hoard them.'

'You will have to do the best you could,' he say with a note of finality.

I can tell you, that of all the Easterners who shelter under my roof, this dozen was the most fantastic and incredible shipment of humanity that I ever set eyes upon. I did think I had a nightmare in the Persian market before Faizull come, but that was a dream of delight. The nightmare was now happening for true. It is hard enough to try and fathom one or two with their dark, scowling faces, piercing resentful eyes, and their general inscrutable miens and bearings. When you are faced with a dozen of the best, closely packed together; when is not only men but woman too – three females was there; when it have a babe-in-arms too (that make twelve and a half, my monetary instinct quickly calculate); when is after midnight and you are in London, a civilized capital metropolis where you do not expect such things to happen – need I go on, dear R? Can you blame me for my tremulous voice and my hollow laughter? Can you blame me if I saw this cluster of beings as in a blur, unable to distinguish one from the other?

'There is no god but Allah,' I mutter under my breath, giving myself some solacement, 'and Mohammed is his prophet.'

Bob wade through the crowd like a white man on safari striding through a recalcitrant mob of native bearers.

'Good gracious,' he say, 'what's this then? What are all these people doing here?'

'I was just telling Faizull we cannot cope,' I say.

Faizull was still acting nervously. This was the first delivery that I ever see him look so uneasy and restless, and it was getting

72

contagious.

'Don't keep them standing here,' he say. 'They have not slept for two nights.'

'Correction,' I say. 'Three nights, because I don't know where they will rest their heads tonight.'

'We must have a talk, Moses,' Faizull say. 'Put them all in Bob's room for a few minutes while we discuss the matter.'

So that's what we do, although it had a overspill and some was standing on the landing, with the door to the room open. Give the devil his due, these orientals didn't make any noise, they didn't say a word, just shuffle into Bob's room – gentlemen first, of course, the women making up the overspill. Clive of India would of been proud to see their docile, servile behaviour. If to say that was a dozen hustlers from the Caribbean, I do not have to tell you they would of started to make rab and kick up rarse long time.

Bob start to tea-trek, using cup and glass and milk bottle and anything that would hold a cuppa, while Faizull and me sit down at the table to sort out the confusion.

'It's impossible,' I start off with.

Faizull haul out a wad of sterling, lick his thumb and start counting.

'You can't make me change my mind with a show of filthy lucre,' I say stoutly – I mean weakly. 'I have no place to keep them. Two or three is okay, but when you start bringing in a battalion, it is a horse of a different colour.'

'I can't dally,' Faizull say. 'I have to be out of London tonight. I have to get rid of the van quickly. Listen carefully to your instructions. They are not to leave the house under any circumstances. In two or three days, we shall be taking them away – not all at once, but in little groups. It may be sooner, and we might be able to cart the lot off together – it just depends on luck. When we have gotten rid of them, you will never see me again.'

'How will I live without you?' I say. But I never have much luck with my sarcasms.

'And if I were you,' he went on, 'I would forget everything that has happened. Just carry on your life as usual.'

'You don't have to remind me,' I say. 'But how do I know for sure that this is the end?'

Faizul was sipping a cup of hot tea and it seem to make him sweat even more.

'I told you the trail is hot,' he say. 'It is in our own interests to function in another different locale.'

'Try to be reasonable, Faizull,' I plead. 'What do you expect me to do with all these people? We would have to slaughter a flock of sheep to feed them.'

'Paki will take care of all the petty details,' he say. 'Leave all that to him.'

As he mention Paki I get an inspiration. 'How about allocating some of them in Paki's room?'

Faizull shake his head. 'No. It won't work out. He is very difficult to live with, being an Untouchable.'

'Then there is no solution,' I say in despair.

Bob brought me a cup of tea.

'How are they getting on?' I ask anxiously, remembering the time when the two infidels did catapult Paki out of the room.

'They are practising segregation already,' he said sadly. 'They are standing around in little groups glaring at each other. I took some milk for the baby, but the mother is breast-feeding it. Right there, in front of everybody. What is to be done, Moses?'

Faizull answer for me. 'They are definitely here for the night,' he say firmly. 'We are planning to get a big house in the country, where new arrivals can lay low.'

'That's all well and good,' I say, 'but it does not solve the immediate problem.'

'How would you like to be in charge of the country house?' Faizull ask me. 'You will double what you are getting now. You and your friend,' he nod at Bob. 'It is always good to have a white man around, it allays suspicion.'

'I appreciate your offer, but I'm afraid we'll have to decline,' I say. 'I cannot wait for the day when I regain my freedom.'

'You chaps from the West Indies are always full of talk,' he sneer. 'You go around as if you were worldly-wise and sophisticated, but when it comes to the crunch and there is a big deal, you chicken out.'

'Don't get racial, Faizull,' I say. 'We have conducted our business so far irregardless of race, colour or creed, in serenity

74

and amicability. And don't change the subject. Where are we going to house these people?'

'You are creating a problem when there is none,' he say, waving his hand airily in the air, encompassing the penthouse.

I do not have to tell you, gentle and perspicacious R, what was being suggested in that significant gesture.

▲ ▲ ▲ ▲

Bob and me had was to walk up the Bayswater road, being as it was too late for bus or tube. Bob had his stripe pyjamas fold up under his arm, and he was in a evil, ranting mood. All I had was this piece of hardboard with a heavy clip on the top holding down my precious annotations. I get in the habit of travelling all about with it, like a trigger-happy photographer waiting for some catastrophy to happen and he would go click click and sell the pictures to the newspapers.

'This is ridiculous, Moses,' Bob rant. 'Furthermore, it is utterly fantastic and unbelievable. If someone came to me relating similar circumstances I would call him a born liar.'

I was not exactly hilarious, either. But you know how sometimes when two people in the same mood, how one try to be the opposite? So I was falling back on some philosophical reflections to sustain me in these desperate hours.

'It is only for the rest of the night,' I say. 'Tomorrow we will have to make some sort of arrangements.'

'Indeed,' Bob say. 'But look at our situation now. A landlord and his lackey wandering the streets, having given up their rooms to a bunch of illegal immigrants.'

'It is certainly a unique situation,' I agree. 'But there is no need to lose your cool.It does not help matters.'

'So what are we going to do, sleep in the park?'

'Don't be absurd,' I say. Though if push come to shove, it was not such a remote possibility. But I was remembering my early immigrant days when I sheltered many a destitute out of the kindness of my heart. Where were they now? Not a one of them could I think of, but Galahad. It hurt me that I had to go and beg him to sleep in his basement room in Bayswater. But surely he would recall those days of yore, when hungry, lonely and sleepy,

75

he came a'knocking and I fed and clothed him, and gave him the old armchair to sleep in.

'We will go to Galahad's room,' I tell Bob.

He made a grimace of distaste. 'That filthy basement!'

'Don't be scornful, Bob,' I chide him. 'I myself started in that selfsame room, and beggars can't be choosers. Don't forget a lot of great English people come from humble surroundings.'

'I prefer the park,' Bob say. 'It's a hot summer's night, and we may find a vacant bench. It's healthier than breathing the foul air in that basement.'

'Sleeping in the park has dreadul connotations of poverty,' I objected. 'We may be homeless tonight, but let's don't behave like hippies and drop-outs.'

And so we wend our way to Galahad's pad, and in truth, descending those basement steps, buffeted by a powerful stench from the dustbins, I had half a mind to turn back and look for a vacancy in Kensington gardens. Besides, I wasn't quite sure what sort of story I was going to tell Galahad. I did already tell Bob to let me do all the talking.

A twenty-watt light went on when we rap the door, and Galahad come and open it. He didn't look surprise or anything. He just stand there in his drawers scratching his testicles.

'What are you doing here at this hour, Moses?' he ask.

'Looking for a place to sleep,' I say. 'Me and Bob.'

Galahad laugh as if is a joke. 'What happen, you bankrupt?'

'Have you got anybody with you?' I ask.

'No. Come in. It so hot I wasn't sleeping.'

We went inside and Bob sit in the armchair, and I sit on the edge of the bed, and Galahad lay back down on the pillow.

'What happen, you get put out?' He was enjoying himself. You know how sometimes you could sense a person in trouble, and it make you feel good that it ain't you, and you not in a hurry to find out, you know that by and by the sufferer will tell his tale of woe. So Galahad hunch up at the head of the bed looking at Bob and me with a smile of contentment and anticipation.

'It's a long story,' I say. I was longing to talk to somebody. I was wondering if I should take him into my confidence and confess the whole affair. A man-about-town like him might have some useful ideas.

76

'Can I sleep in this armchair?' Bob ask in an aggressive tone.

'Sure.' Galahad wave his hand and dismiss Bob. Bob start to take off his clothes and put on his pyjamas, muttering to himself.

Galahad light up a cigarette and put a empty matchbox next to him for ashtray.

Bot went out to pee and come back.

'The toilet is blocked,' he say, holding his nose.

'Use a milk bottle,' Galahad say, and turn to me. 'Let's hear the ballad.'

So I tell Galahad everything. I thought I might as well, because I didn't think I could sleep again that night. At the end of my narrative, Galahad look thoughtful and say, 'Twenty pounds a head, eh?'

'It's all your fault for critizing my Memoirs,' I say bitterly. 'And now the matter has snowballed into its present state.'

'Twenty pounds a head, eh?' he say, 'can you put me in touch with Farouk?'

'I expect you to commiserate with me in this devilish predicament, not think of lining your own pockets,' I say angrily.

'I do, I do,' Galahad say sincerely. 'But seeing that you will be going out of business, as it were, couldn't you recommend me to look after that house in the country for them?' And he started to list off his qualifications, not least of which was that he was a militant and any move from the law to blockade the traffic would lead to blood and sand. 'In fact,' he concluded, 'these Pakis do not know their arse from their elbow, not knowing the lingo. They need a man like me. I like that one about you asking if he speakee English and he say fuck you.' And Galahad leaned back and laugh kiff-kiff, scratching his testicles again.

Sauce for the goose isn't sauce for the gander, so I say to him that once that dirty dozen quit my premises, I will be through with the organization lock, stock and barrel.

'You will still have Paki as a tenant, though,' Galahad say.

'I will endeavour to let him straggle after the others,' I retorted.

'Don't act hastily,' Galahad say, 'he might be useful if you want to get in touch with the gang for any reason. Twenty pounds a head, eh?' He couldn't get the blood money out of his mind. 'That means you have two hundred and fifty pounds on the hoof, in a manner of speaking.' And he chuckle, as if he like the way he talk.

'There's a wee tot too,' I say, trying my sarcasm, to no avail. 'In a roundabout way, Galahad, you have caused this impasse.'

'Don't accuse me, I never told you anything about those bloody Pakis,' he rejoined. 'I meant Our People. If you had stuck to your own kind, you wouldn't of been in this shit. Listen to me, Moses. I can give you enough ballad and episode to full ten books.'

'I follow your advice once,' I say, 'and look where it got me.'

'You got yourself there, boy,' he chuckle. 'Not through altruism either. Sterlingism, more likely. Twenty pounds a head is not to be sneezed at in these days of sugar shortage.'

'We'll never see eye-to-eye,' I say wearily.

'I tell you again,' he say, 'that if you want to pursue your so-called memoirs, you only have to interview the first black man you meet on the street.'

'I will knock them in the Old Kent Road with my language alone,' I boast. 'My very usage of English will have them rolling in the aisles. Mark my words, Galahad.'

'Shit,' Galahad say shortly, and hawk into the fireplace. Lucky thing Bob was asleep. 'You are living high off the hog's back and it has addled your brains.'

Bob was snoring gently. Every time we stop talking, he stop snoring too; I don't know if it was deliberate or not.

I felt I had to say something, so I say, 'Judging that you have made no progress yourself, I don't see what I can get from others of your ilk.'

'Don't mind me,' he say. 'I live menially because I give all my money to the cause, unlike some of us, who buy houses and aspire to live above their standards. I can switch you on to top level people as becomes your rank.'

I sort of stretch out on the edge of the bed, trying out a tentative position for sleep without touching Galahad. It was a single bed, and I remember it used to collapse with the weight of two people struggling on it, and I could never enjoy a stroke in comfort when I haul in a sleeper. Galahad, as if he read my thoughts, say, 'I tussle on the ground, man, if I manage to haul a thing in,' and he shift up to the wall to give me a little space.

Smelling them basement smells as they combine with Galahad sour sweat, remind me of the fable that English people broadcast that we smell more than them. I agree that black people have an odour, but I contend that it is an earthy aroma because of their constant toil against the odds. It is that rank sweatiness you get when the labourer comes in from the fields, having done an honest day's work. As to the smell of white people in general, and the English in particular, I cannot say the same. I must say that I have had to encourage, goad, and even order Bob to have a bath. What he used to do was to have a dry-clean – as he humorously tried to call his uncleanliness – using a dirty washing rag rub up in soap under the neck, behind the ears, under the arms, and finish off with a dash of Woolworths talcum powder. I found it disgusting, and told him so, but that was the way he was brought up. You only have to smell some of these temporary and permanent secretaries and typists in the rush hour in the tube to know what I mean. You get a whiff of them frowsy English girls what look sharp on the outside but ain't changed their panties and bras for weeks, and only cover up the day-before perspiration with another layer of talcum and a quick splash of water on their face. Once, in this selfsame basement room, I haul in a posh sleeper who say she was doing a big work in the Houses of Parliament, but that she was out for kicks, and that was why she pretended to allow me to lead her to Bayswater. Well, to cut a long story short, while I was sucking her nipples, I find something crunchy in my mouth. 'What's this?' I ask her with disgust, spitting it out. She giggled, 'I didn't wash today,' she say, as if that make her more desirable. When I investigated the flakes I spat out, I found it was vintage talcum which had calcified that she was hoarding as if a shortage was threatened. That was the upper regions; I will not disgust you further by my encounter with the lower regions. Suffice it to say that I forgot her real name but always thought of it as 'Crusty.'

I look around the room – it barely have space to swivel your eyeballs – at the wallpaper falling off and bringing down bits of ancient plaster with it, and splatter up with grease and food stains near the fireplace; on the table a dirty cup and saucer, with cigarette butts and ashes in the saucer, and a plate and spoon with coagulated stew gravy and a few grains of rice. I didn't think

I could sleep even if I wanted to. I was trying hard to avoid any physical contact with Galahad's sweating body; I myself was beginning to feel moist under the armpits. He was smoking again and muttering to himself, 'Twenty pounds a head, eh,' as if he doing some heavy mental calculations, though he had a finger on the wall writing invisible figures to help him. I could see he was planning to hire the Queen Mary and transport the entire population of Pakistan to the shores of Brit'n.

All these things was like another nightmare. You does find yourself wondering if white people does live like this, and have similar experiences. When I was a little boy in Trinidad, the old ones use to tell the children to try and live and behave like white people, and I used to imagine that white people live in Paradise, and it was so nice there that they didn't want no black people to enter and muddy up the water, because they wouldn't know how to comport themselves and appreciate the goodies. Now, Galahad was taking a turn in my arse for trying to better my living conditions. I know fully well what he was after. You know how some people feel guilty with their wealth and always donating something to charity to salve their conscience? That's what Galahad was after – to make me feel unhappy with my hard-earned money, so I would throw something in the kitty for the Party. But I had no qualms about my worldly possessions. I did start off in this selfsame basement room he was living in now. No one should begrudge me a few creature comforts, least of all Galahad, who witnessed my days of depression and despair. So I didn't bother with him. Mark you, appertaining to my Memoirs, perhaps a little scouting amongst the black citizens might prove fruitful, and I had it at the back of my mind to undertake same as soon as I got the Pakis off my hands.

▲ ▲ ▲ ▲

None of this narrative is fiction: if I lie I die. It might sound so, but I can't help if people in this city does live in a dream world and refuse to believe or accept the things that happen under their very noses. When the mark bust they are shocked and dismayed to discover what is going on, but pass it over with alacrity to resume their traditional and comforting equanimity and poise.

That's what I had in mind, too: but easier said than done. When I went back home the next day, I couldn't even get into the penthouse. The occupants lock the door from the inside, and wouldn't open up.

I went to see Paki.

'Look man,' I say, 'I can't even get into my own room.'

'They are very suspicious and frightened,' Paki say. 'Faizull told them not to open the door to anyone but myself, and to hear is to obey.'

I wandered about the house trying doors. All the other tenants gone to work, and Bob wasn't here, and he had the spare set of keys. I went down to the basement. If the Pakis usurp me, at least I had Our People in the basement, and might be able to raise a cup of tea with Brenda.

But down there I find I was only in the way as Sister Brenda and her assistants conducted their affairs. She busy on a old Remington typewriter, and the two chaps with she was sorting out a pile of circulars.

I didn't get so much as the time of day until Brenda happen to glance up and see me standing there.

'Hello Moses,' she say grudgingly, 'what can I do for you?'

'You can clear out of my house with your militant Black Power friends,' I imagine myself saying. But what I say is: 'I want to see you.'

'We are very busy, Moses. Let me finish this letter, Grab a seat.'

I sit down gratefully. I feel as if I was in one of them scruffy office you find all over London, when two or three chaps open up a company to beat the Income Tax. But you couldn't mistake this one for anything but what it was. It had pictures of Joe Louis, Marcus Garvey, Louis Armstrong, Malcom X, Malcolm Z, and a host of other black heroes. And slogans stick up all over: FIGHT THE GOOD FIGHT and I AM A BLACK MAN, WHO ARE YOU?

'Why don't you assist the boys while you're waiting?' Brenda suggest. 'Put some of those circulars into envelopes.'

'How much you paying?' I ask.

She look shock. 'Everything is voluntary here,' she say. 'Those who work do so because they are aware of the Winds of Change, and Third World potentialities.'

'Third World,' I say mournfully. 'It hard enough to live in one, and you-all making three.'

'Apathy is our greatest enemy,' Brenda say, forgetting the typing to rap about her heart's delight. 'If you don't stand up and be counted, you will be swept away.'

She put the letter in a envelope and lick the flap.

You'd better go and post this now,' she say to one of the auxiliaries. 'I want to catch the midday post.'

She put another sheet of paper in the machine. I feel like a prisoner in my own house. I didn't know if I was better off twiddling my thumbs in the basement, or lurking in the hallway upstairs to see if one of the refugees would come out and give me a chance to put my foot in the doorway. It look as if Fate had me shuttling 'tween Pakis and blacks, and I thought that while I was down here I might as well avail myself of the opportunity to do some research.

'Sister,' I say earnestly to Brenda, 'how does the struggle fare? Are we really making any headway against the fuzz and the pigs from Babylon?'

Brenda look up and smile pitifully. 'You mean the police?'

'Yes. Why you call them Babylon?'

'Read your Bible and you'll find out.'

I wait until she type a few words then I heave a great sigh. 'I have not been pulling my weight,' I say. I would like to make amends.'

'You're seeing the light of day?' she ask.

'Yes. What qualifications do I have to have in order to join the Party?'

'Your blackness entitles you to membership,' she say, stopping the typing. 'It is a universal struggle, Moses. As long as you are black, no matter what part of the world you are in, you belong to the brotherhood.'

'It got no white people in the Party, then?'

'Sure we've got some well-wishers and do-gooders, but not many.' She look at me. 'You really want to join?'

'But you just said I am already a member.'

'Ah, yes, but you do nothing. You have expressed views of indifference and withdrawal. You do not even attend a meeting.'

82

'When is the next one?'

'There's a speaker from the Black Panthers of America at the youth centre tonight.'

'Get a ticket for me.'

'You don't need no bloody ticket, man! You just come along, like any interested black citizen.'

'I suppose there will be a collection?'

'I knew you'd come to that,' she say disgustedly. 'Those who have give. Right at this moment we are trying to raise money to defend a brother who has wrongfully been accused of possessing drugs. I don't suppose you care to make a donation as an earnest of your intentions?'

'Give me some time to acquaint myself with the Party's activities,' I say. 'When I am satisfied that all is bona fide, I will come big.'

'You are full of words, Moses,' she say, 'but I like you.'

Right then the door knock and Paki look in.

'I want to see you, Moses,' he say.

'I will be with you in a tick,' I say.

'Tell me something,' Brenda say when he went away, 'have you got Indian blood?'

'Not that I know of,' I say.

'I've noticed a predominance of orientals in the house of late.'

'They come and go,' I say truthfully.

'Oh, they don't bother me,' she say, 'I just wondered.'

I left Brenda and went up to Paki. 'Can I enter my room now?' I ask.

'You'll get a chance when I go up to feed them,' he say. 'I need a hand.'

I didn't live and work in Brit'n all these years for nothing. I smile. 'I belong to a union,' I say, 'that's not part of my duties.'

'I can't leave them alone,' Paki say. 'I want you to be here while I go out to the take-away restaurant and bring back the food. Unless you go for the food yourself?'

I debate in my mind which was the lesser of two evils, 'I think I'll go for the food.'

'You're sure?' Paki say doubtfully. 'It's a rather mixed order. Some of them are vegetarians. Some don't eat meat. Some eat meat but not pork. Some eat pork but no beef. And you've got to get each item in a separate bag. Have a look at this list,' and he hand me a piece of paper.

This is what I see:

1) Mughlai Biryani
2) Yakhni Pulao
3) Murgh Musallam
4) Mutton do Pyaza
5) Sanitary napkins (cheap ones)
6) Hussaini Curry
7) Roghan Josh
8) Chicken Vindaloo
9) One tin Cow and Gate Milk
10) Shami Kabab
11) Bengali Machher Jhol
12) Escalopes de Veau à l'Oseille
13) Toad in the Hole
14) Fish and Chips

'What's fish and chips?' I ask.

'That's what I mean,' he say. 'You won't understand. I'd better go. I won't be long.'

While he was away I took the opportunity to look around the room, but there was no incriminating evidence about. I was taking a look at my notes and making some changes when there was a timid knock at the door. I open it and see one standing there. This was a predicament I had not foreseen. He bend and look around to see if Paki was in the room. Then he straighten up and look at me with a poker face.

'Speakee English?' I venture warily, remembering Paki's pungent retort that other time.

'Fish and chips,' he say.

'Can I help you?' I ask.

'Fish and chips,' he say.

It look like he wanted to play a game. 'Egg and bacon?' I crack.

'Fish and chips,' he say.

'Oh come off it,' I say. Then it dawn on me that he wanted to find out what was happening to the food. 'Paki's gone to get it.'

He gave me a walloping thump in the chest. 'Fish and chips,' he say. God alone knows how long Paki had been starving the poor souls. He must of been diverting some of the funds Faizull left him as expenses. I had that thought as I straighten up after his wallop.

'Is that all you can say,' I snarled. 'I told you. Paki will be back in a few minutes.'

He shake his head sympathetically, like when you trying to explain something to a foreigner and he can't understand. 'Chips and fish,' he said slowly, permutating the phrase.

'Oh fuck off,' I say, paying him back in Paki's coin.

His eyes narrowed. He was a big burly chap, and he had on a turban what make him look taller still, and a hairnet over his beard which stop it from bristling. He held my shoulders and gave me a shake. I don't know what would of happened if Paki didn't return at that moment. He say something angrily to F-and-C, and he let hold of me and went back upstairs.

'Sorry about that,' Paki tell me. 'I had to go to more than one restaurant to get the food.' He put down about six big plastic carriers on the table carefully, though some of them already had the telltale, yellow signs of curry. 'Faizull is taking away a few this evening.' I don't know if he was consoling himself or me. 'Women and children first. I will try to squeeze what's left into Bob's room, so you can get your place.'

'I don't see why you can't accommodate them here,' I say.

Paki look at me as if I mad. 'There is no god but Allah,' he say. 'I would rather die. Bad enough that I have to look after them.' He pick some bags off the table. 'Help me to take these upstairs.'

I pick up the food and follow Paki. What else I could do, pray?

We went to Bob room first, and dole out the women. I didn't see which one pick up the mensing pads, Paki just left them on the table with the Cow and Gate.

Then we went up to the others. Paki knock and say something that sound like opensesame, but it could of been my imagination. By the time the door open I dash straight in and went to the cupboard where I had my Memoirs. Praise the Lord – I mean Allah – it was intact. Only then I look around to see the state the rest of the penthouse was in, and the disposition of the occupants.

85

Everything was push up to one wall, to make a big space wherein the adventurers were squatting, kneeling, or just downright sitting on the carpet. Three was facing East, salaaming Mecca. One was facing the opposite wall, as if he misbehave in class and the teacher put him there. Another was crouch up with his two hands clasp together as if he playing a mouth-organ, but on closer inspection he was smoking, putting the cigarette to his nostril and exhaling through his mouth. Another was standing on his head getting a worm's eye view of things. (I tell you one thing – these orientals full of gimmicks, you see, it would not of surprised me to find one of them climbing up a piece of rope, or blowing a flute and bringing out a king cobra from a basket.) They did rig up a clothes line right across the room, and it was full up of saris, turbans, fezzes, dhotis, poshteens, lungis, shantungs, caftans, and other oriental items of dress what I had to look up in the dictionary afterwards. Nevertheless, I reckon things could of been much worse. I would have to wait until they evacuate to make a proper inventory, but from what I could see at the moment they did not run amok and cry havoc.

Paki and F-and-C was having a argument over the food which was spread out on the table. The others desert their meditations and prayers and cluster around, inspecting the dishes as closely as they could without a microscope. Each one take his order and went off in a corner to eat by himself. I stop a chap who was taking the fish and chips.

'That's his,' I say, pointing to F-and-C.

But that worthy was already dipping his hands in the vindaloo. I went into the kitchen to make myself a ham sandwich, leaving Paki opening cans and bottles of beer. He followed me shortly, with his own can.

'What will happen to these people once they leave this house?' I ask.

Paki take a swig and shrug. 'We get them here. After that it's up to them.'

He sound more communicative than Faizull, so I follow up with: 'How does the system work?'

But I jump the gun. Paki smile and say, 'Naughty, naughty. The less you know, the better off you are.'

'You want a ham sandwich?' I offer.

'Okay,' he say, sitting on the kitchen stool and swinging his legs.

I made him a sandwich and he start eating with gusto.

'Don't you have any of them Musallam and Escalopes?' I ask.

'Don't make me laugh,' he say.

'Have you ever met Farouk?' I ask next, seeing that abrupt, random questions was in vogue.

'Who's he?' he ask.

'You know. Faizull's friend who was staying here with him.'

'Oh that.' Paki give a big grin. 'That was a good idea – I suppose I could tell you, now that operations are going to cease in this locality.'

But he didn't continue immediately. Drama isn't the monopoly of Shakespeare's people, as you have already seen. He fidget and shift his position, and then, casually, 'Farouk doesn't exist.'

'He was a tenant in this house,' I protest.

'Faizull established two identities as a security measure,' Paki say leisurely.

I did not fall off a tree, as some nincompoops. 'Say no more,' I say, 'I was taken for a sleigh ride in July.'

'A man of your wit,' he scoffed. 'I thought you knew all the time. His full name is Faizull Farouk.'

Well, though the disclosure took me down a peg or two, I will not make a song and dance about it, lest you think I am lying and pick holes in my story. If I lie I die.

'There is no god but *the* god,' I say staunchly. 'How are the others getting on?'

'Let's go and see,' he say, swinging off the stool.

I did not see any point in being finicky about mixing now that I was inside; after all, they would soon be citizens like myself and we would all have to *integrade*. Besides, if the women went I wanted to make sure the men went down to Bob's room, and I told Paki this.

They didn't take kindly to the idea – sweetened up, I suppose, by the penthouse – F-and-C especially start up a harangue with Paki pointing to me and shaking his head.

'What's up?' I ask Paki.

'They won't go to Bob's room,' Paki explain. 'They think he is a skinhead, and they would be bashed.'

'Nonsense,' I cry. 'Bob is with us.'

'This chap,' Paki point to F-and-C, 'wants to know if you are a Christian?'

'Tell him I am of the Faith,' I say, 'and that I am bloody well staying put now that I am in here. If it is any consolation to them, I am going into my bedroom and will stay there until Faizull comes.'

And speaking my piece as the landlord, I stormed out of their presence, and ensconced myself in the bedroom.

▲ ▲ ▲ ▲

Faizull pull up in front of the house in the selfsame big removal van, earlier than I expected. It was the rush hour, in fact. I did think he would wait for nightfall to shift them, but he explained that there was less danger moving around at that hour, when everybody was hustling to get home and the traffics snarl-up.

There is a change of plan,' he say. 'I will have to take the lot.'

'All of them?'

'Yes.'

'This is goodbye, then?'

'I'm afraid so.'

'There is no god but Mohammed,' I say fervently, 'and Allah is his prophet.'

'There's hope for you yet,' Faizull say approvingly.

I cannot express my feelings as my guests folded their bundles, wrapped their belongings, donned their turbans and saris, gave the tot a double dose of Cow and Gate, and made other preparations for the evacuation. Was it sadness or gladness? Did I long to learn a trick or two from them, like eating a bottle which I saw F-and-C do for his dessert? Did I yearn to learn a few phrases of their exotic language, so that if the tables were ever turned and Britons were immigrating to Pakistan, and I had to be amongst them, I could tell my host to fuck off in Urdu? Was I, perhaps, subconsciously forsaking Christianity to answer the call of the muezzin? All I know is that I experienced a welter of emotions as I moved among them, helping to tie a parcel here,

88

tucking in a turban there. In the midst of all this Bob returned from some casual labour.

'Ah,' he beamed, 'we're getting rid of the lot, eh?'

'How can you be so heartless?' I say. 'Their worries are now beginning when they are let loose on the British public.'

Faizull came to us. 'I wish Bob would go away,' he say. 'They cannot get it out of their minds that he is a skinhead and liable to bash them.'

'I wish I had thought of that before,' Bob say regretfully.

'Go out in the road Bob,' I tell him, 'and stay there and make sure the coast is clear as they leave the house.'

Faizull did a last round-up and five-thirty – I mean seventeen-thirty – precisely, the first batch of three went out to the van, and thereafter, at intervals of three minutes, the others followed.

I stood by the window of the penthouse, observing the exodus, a lump in my throat. Those of you who take up your cudgels against these poor unfortunates, who lobby the House of Commons and write letters to Members of Parliament, who march in protest waving banners and shouting imprecations on their heads, cannot understand my mixed emotions. I stood there counting them as they entered the van. Twenty pounds, forty, sixty – and when I turned away, there was a tear in my eye.

The last to leave was F-and-C, and I could not bear the thought that he might be going with enmity in his heart against me, and I would never see him again once he was swallowed up in the London jungle.

I dashed downstairs and caught him just as he was entering the van.

'Let's be friends,' I say proffering my hand, 'I wish you the best of British luck during your stay in our country.'

He shook my hand warmly and say, 'Fuck-off.'

Only one day in Brit'n, and he was already picking up the language.

▲ ▲ ▲ ▲

Bob and me clean up the place as best we could. To tell you the truth it was not in such a bad state. There was a lingering smell of incense we could not dispel with any of the aero sprays, and one

89

of Bob's sheets had bloodstains on it. But it could of been worse, I tell him, let us count our blessings, and our ill-gotten gains.

Later, sitting down with cans of chilled beer – they didn't touch one thing in the fridge, and Bob say they must of been afraid of contamination, but I prefer to think it was the goodness of their hearts – I try to inveigle Bob to come with me to the Black Power meeting.

'Good lord,' he say, 'haven't you had enough? We have just been through a harrowing experience. You must have sufficient notes to fill your book.'

'I don't think so,' I say. 'Gentle readers might be disappointed that I did not hop in the van and go along to record their further adventures. If I do some circulation among the blacks, it will mitigate their disappointment.'

'You have allowed Galahad to influence you,' Bob accuse.

'That's true,' I admit, 'but I can't continue as I started.'

'I don't know where you're getting this sudden energy from,' he grumble. 'Hitherto you were content to recline here and take it easy. Can't you work with Brenda in the basement and make your notes?'

'That is too prosaic,' I say. 'I have to get out there in London, where the action is. I must be on the spot when blood flow.'

It might be your blood. Remember what happened in Trafalgar Square.'

'I have to take risks. According to Galahad there is a vast store of materials just waiting to be tapped by someone like me. Come on, Bob, I will share my royalties with you.'

Thus persuaded, Bob decide to come along with me to this place in North Kensington. It was not a healthy neighbourhood to be in, especially at night, and I was glad of his company.

When we get there the first one we see is Galahad.

'Well come and welcome,' he say, giving me a wink. 'Brenda has cautioned me that you want to join the ranks.'

'I only want to reconnoitre the set-up,' I tell him. 'We'll see about joining up later.'

'That's prudent,' Galahad say, 'Cool your heels, the meeting will start in a few minutes.'

Bob and me had a chance to look around, but it don't have much to describe. I always find these community centres and club rooms and church halls depressing. It's always some stale building, with a lot of space and second-hand furniture strewn about, and a ping-pong table with a collapsing net, and obvious attempts to slap on a heavy coat of paint to cover flaws in the walls, and a notice board with forthcoming events and reminders to pay your sub. You get the feeling that it's just a desperate alternative to roaming the streets.

By the time the meeting was about to start, it had about fifty people there, not including the circulating Party members, nor those already ensconced on the platform with the Black Panther. And some more was still coming in. I must say I was favourably impressed to see so many. You might not think it's a lot, but unless it have free food and drinks and raggae music, it's hard to amass a black crowd.

Galahad say, when I mention this, 'Sometimes we have even more. You see how conscious people are becoming of the struggle?'

'I note some whites in our midst,' I say.

'Friends of the Party,' he say. 'Staunch supporters.'

Me and Bob take a back seat, near to the exit in case the gathering get too restive and enthusiastic. Besides, Bob had a flask of whisky in his jacket pocket, from which we was taking surreptitious sips. He was half-charge already, and was reaching the mellow stage where he couldn't care less if he was in the Albert Hall or Galahad basement room.

Galahad call the meeting to order, and say how proud and happy the committee was that they was able to bring the Black Panther to the people of North Kensington, all the more reason since BP was a very busy man, and during his short stay in Brit'n would be travelling all over the country with a two-fold purpose; A, to meet the brothers and sisters and inform them that the American contingent was looking on with an approving eye on how the black people of Brit'n was pulling their weight; and B, to spread the gospel to the white heathens, as he, BP, was also a man of God, and he had come to the conclusion that the crux of the matter was that not enough black missionaries like himself infiltrated the white jungles, 'and I will now call upon Sister Brenda to say a few words about our activities in this zone, before our august visitor takes the floor.'

91

Sister Brenda say that she know that the audience didn't come here tonight to hear she nor Galahad rap, but BP, but she just wanted to remind them how the Party was growing from strength to strength, that when they first started they had nothing at all but belief and determination, and now they had an office and was going to start up a newspaper what would tell the people the truth and not no pack of lies you read in the English press nor see and hear on the television, but they desperately needed the support of the community, because words and ideals was useless unless everyone put their hands in their pockets, and she didn't mean to scratch their balls, but to take them out with currency (laughter), and she could go on and on and tell us of all the things the Party had done, but she won't, as she knew that everyone was sitting on the edges of their seats to hear BP, who was not only the active President of the American brigade, but also a messenger of God, 'so without further ado, brothers and sisters, I give you BP.'

I will say this much for our visitor from the States, that he wasn't dress up in Black Power paraphernalia nor armoury, but in a nice dark gaberdine suit. He was a tall panther, with a little beard, and every now and then, whilst he speaking, he lift up his chin to show us the beard. First, he blow into the microphone, and then adjust it to his height.

'Brothers and sisters,' he begin, 'let us pray.' He went on to say that we was not praying for ourselves so much, because the ears of God was already deaf with the black man's supplications, but he was directing his appeal for the other side, because if our enemies were converted to the ways of Christ, he was sure they would act as human beings. Nevertheless, he say, if we can't get justice and humanity through Christianity, we would have to resort to the sword, and he was sorry to say it, but that white blood would flow like water ere we attained our rightful desires. He tell us what the panthers doing in America, and how they appreciate the participation of their English brothers and sisters. One of the audience interrupt to say that we was not English, nor treated as such, nor recognized as such. Galahad, on guard against hecklers, hastily explained that what brother BP had in mind was a terminology only, and nothing personal was intended. BP continued to say how words were fine, but he reckoned action was better, and the Party was a good example of getting things done, you cats really know how to get moving.

I did not know how all this was going to help my Memoirs, but I was scribbling away like mad. Bob finish the flask, hiccup gently and put it down on the floor and give it a quiet kick to slide it under the chair in front of him.

BP was now working himself up for the big crescendo to electrify and whip the audience into a frenzy, which all black politicians love to do when they have the chance. I don't rightly recollect the context leading up to it, but suddenly he was screaming out to kill all the whites and burn down the City of London, and as far as the pigs were concerned, hang one up in the doorway of every police station.

He was now cooking with gas and the crowd begin to stamp and cheer and make the sign of the fist in the air, and shout and sing We Shall Overcome, Black is Beautiful, and Onward Christian Soldiers, and some of them already on their feet to go into battle instantaneously.

BP wipe sweat off his forehead with a white handkerchief, and was about to sit down when Galahad whisper something in his ear. He went back to the mike and raise his hands calling for order. When the crowd begin to quieten down, he say that he was sure we would all show our true colours by donating something to the Party, and he for one was going to speak to the Treasurer of the Black Panthers of America as soon as he got back and see that something substantial cross the Atlantic to help the strugglers on this side. Furthermore, he was going to set the ball a-rolling right now, cats, and so saying, he take out a crumpled American dollar from his pocket, and look at it thoughtfully for a few moments, keeping everybody in suspense. Then he smooth it out and with much pomp and pageantry, to the blast of imagined trumpets and bugles, he hand it to Sister Brenda as if he handing over the rights to Fort Knox. (I questioned Galahad about this magnaminous gift some time later, and he explained that BP did not want to embarrass the audience by making a great show of American Aid by flashing notes of greater denomination, for fear that they would be abashed to contribute their new pence.)

Brenda and Galahad come off the platform and start to circulate amongst the audience taking the collection, making facetious remarks like every bit helps as the actress said to the bishop, and that they have change if anybody want to change a fiver.

When Brenda come by me I try to make a deferred payment like BP, but she stand up there until I put my hand in my pocket and give her ten pee. At least I thought it was ten pee, but Brenda look at it and exclaim, 'Fifty pee! Can you afford it?'

'Hold on,' I say, 'I thought it was ten pee. Give me some change.' But she only laugh and pass on. Since this new currency come to Brit'n, it was the first time that my fingers ever mistake a fifty pee for a ten pee. The only consolation I had was that it was better it went to the brotherhood rather than in some white man pocket.

It would be catholic if I could say that at the meeting chaps was smoking weed or making too much noise or any reason you can think of to explain the sudden appearance of a battalion of Babylon. But I would swear to God, and kiss the Bible, that I witness no misdemeanour or untowardliness going on in the hall, and that when the blood-thirsty Alsatians were let loose, and when I see defenders of the law charging in to attack, I was completely flabbergasted. Suddenly Last Summer pandemonium break out and take over from the Party anthem which everybody was singing at the time. The cowards invade from the rear. First there was the Alsatians, and before any of the audience could give them a pat on the head and say 'Good boy, Rover,' the dogs was at their throats, ready for the kill.

I tell you, the whole thing was so unexpected, that I thought it was some gimmick that the Party organize, to show that even animals was on we side. But pigs follow the dogs and people start to jump up and run and kick down chair and flee all over.

I leap on to the platform like a bat out of hell hoping to make an escape in the wings. Sir Galahad was standing bravely there, waving his arms like a tick-tack bookie and shouting, 'Don't panic! Don't panic!'

Don't panic indeed. Everybody was dashing about to get at a safe distance before stopping to ask questions or prove their innocences. I manage to get outside only to see a convoy of police cars park up in the road with them blue lights on the roof going round in circles like a lighthouse, and a pig with a walkie-talkie like he giving a running commentary of proceedings to police headquarters.

I start to walk away from the spectators gathering on the pavement, like a scornful pedestrian who deigns not to exhibit any morbid curiosity.

And at the first crossroads I come to, I start to run.

I run and run, like if the devil was behind me. I run until I couldn't run no more. I try to beat a traffic lights I see at amber ahead of me, but it change to red as soon as I got there, and I stand up panting and breathing like a blacksmith bellows, pressing the pedestrian button frantically. Those of you who perambulate like myself know the frustration and impatience that one suffers under normal circumstances as the traffics flow to and fro while you wait for the little green man to light up and start walking, and like he fall asleep or something. You can imagine my feelings with the added terror of what I left behind me, and as I see a London Weekend Television van speeding to the scene of the crime.

It was only after I cross the zebra, and notice people strolling casually around me, that I slow down and begin to catch my breath and my thoughts.

The latters was in a mess, and numerous. I try to rationalize the situation. Okay. So it must of had some wanted criminals in the hall, in spite of the respectable aspects of the meeting. Right? So the police make a raid and bust up the gathering. Right? That was it, simple and plain. Right?

I catch a bus 52 in Ladbroke Grove and went to Notting Hill Gate and catch a 88 and went home, but I still couldn't convince myself that it was as simple as all that. I was beginning to get vex now; my dignity was affronted as I imagine myself pelting down the road terror-stricken when I didn't do nothing at all, not even spit on the pavement or smoke in a non-smoking compartment. Was all of we in the hall criminals that we had to jump up and flee for our very lives? There we was, sitting down, and I was just writing down the words of the Party anthem, when we was so rudely interrupted. My blood begin to boil. I had half a mind to get back there and ask the Inspector himself what was the meaning of this outrage? 'How dare you intrude on this peaceful gathering,' I would say, 'and strike terror into the hearts of these innocent people?' And I would ask him for his name, number

95

and rank, and report him to the Chief of Scotland Yard.

Whilst I was thus working myself up into a towering rage Bob come home.

'How did the battle fare?' I ask. 'How many dead or wounded?'

'There were many casualties,' Bob say. 'How did you escape?'

'I fled. Ignobly, like a dog with tail 'twixt its legs.'

Bob went to the fridge and get a can of beer and open it and put it to his mouth quick to catch the froth and don't waste any.

'What was it all about?' I ask him. 'Did you find out anything?'

'It appears they were after drugs,' he say. 'They arrested Galahad, Brenda and BP.'

'What for?'

'I don't know, ringleaders, I suppose. I only saw them being bundled into a van and whisked off.'

'I don't understand this, Bob,' I say. 'Why should they do such a thing?'

Bob had a swig, look thoughtful, then say, 'Much against my will, I gravely suspect it is only because they are black. No whites were captured.'

I was thunderstruck. 'God's blood,' I cried, 'they have gone too far this time. To arms!'

'Hold your water,' Bob say. 'Cool it.'

'Cool it?' I mock him. 'Egad, man, they have really irked my ire now. Come, let us away.'

'Away where?'

'To the police station, of course.'

'I don't see what good that will do.'

'They bound to give them bail. We will stand security and get them out.'

'My dear fellow,' Bob began.

'Don't hem and haw, matey,' I say.

'I mean we have barely got shot of the smell of curry and joss sticks, and you want to dabble in black tragic?'

Were the moment different, I might of doffed my hat at that one and make a note to use it.

'These are My People,' I say grimly, 'No Englishman with black blood in his veins can stand aside and see innocent victims hang. We were party to that meeting, Bob. We seen what happen with our own eyes.'

'Aye,' he say, and give a little shudder. 'I saw an Alsatian leap upon a helpless woman and maul her. And Brenda was roughly handled in spite of her womanhood. Two pigs literally hoisted her out of the hall.'

'What are we waiting for?' I cried. 'We should have enough cash in the house. Get it all together and let's make haste.'

It was thus that I became involved in spite of my misgivings and philosophy of neutrality. One would not be worth one's salt to turn a blind eye and a deaf ear to the injustice of that night. I know all the failings and shortcomings of My People, their foibles and chicanery, their apathy and disunity, but I were less than a Pharisee to leave them by the wayside. Such was my righteous indignation that I did not even consider the recoverability of the three hundred pounds, plus twenty-five new pee for stamp duty, that I had to fork out for the brothers and sister. I told Galahad, after their release, that the money could be used for their defence when they bust a case in the police arse for wrongful arrests.

BP promised that when he returned to the States he would get the Panthers to send me a cheque, but I brushed it aside.

'Man,' he say, 'you cats got a great herd of pigs over here. They go around breaking up peaceful meetings as if they were making Custer's Last Stand. I got to watch out for these London bobbies.'

'Inform the brothers over there,' Galahad say. 'Perhaps they do not appreciate that we suffer such atrocities regularly.'

Brenda say, looking at me significantly, 'I hope Brother Moses will honour us with his membership now that he has seen for himself.'

Galahad say, giving me a clap on the shoulder, 'I knew Moses would come round, it was just a question of time. In his heart he was always an honorary member.'

'I wouldn't go so far as to say that,' I say cautiously. 'I remember when I was incarcerated you left me to my doom.'

'We've got thousands of cats like Moses back in the States,' BP say. 'You've got to let them taste the fire for themselves. And man, when they do, they want more fire and blood than we got to give.'

'I am a peaceful man by nature,' I say, now that my ardour was cooling. 'I don't want my participation tonight to be misconstrued. It only came about through researching for my Memoirs.'

'Moses fancy himself as the British Baldwin,' Galahad nudge BP.

'Enough,' I say sternly, 'don't make no *pappyshow* of my ambitions. Being from America, BP would know that some of us can contribute even more than big-mouths like you.'

'You said a mouthful, babe,' BP reply. 'I love you, man. I *dig* you, you know? Cats back home know how important that is – ain't you seen our programmes on the box? We gotta get the kids to read, man, and somebody gotta produce the right books.' He didn't have a cigar in his mouth, but I envisaged him with it. 'How's about me giving you cats a lift in my Mercedes, huh? I got it parked somewhere outside that hall. Unless your pigs towed it away?'

But the pigs did leave it; I guess they couldn't of dreamed that a black man would be driving around in a Mercedes. Maybe a old beat-up Ford, or a 1920 Vauxhall, but a Mercedes, no.

I never drive in such a car before; I was afraid to breathe when we was in it, and it was a pity that it had to be in such distressing circumstances, and not attending the Queen's Garden Party or something.

Him and Galahad went off, ostensibly to plan a campaign with the party committee, a sort of counter-attack against the swines. I say ostensibly because knowing Galahad as I do, I could not see him missing the opportunity of cruising around the West End in BP's Mercedes looking for pussy, pretending to show the American the sights. I've heard it said that when you are mobile you stand a better chance of a pick up. I would not know about that; in my heyday I earned my piece of cunt by the sweat of my brow, plodding the streets of Londontown, and building up courage to tackle a thing, thickening my skin in case you get a nasty rebuff like a colour reference. Galahad would know the routes to drive along, and no doubt there are no flies on these brothers from the States when it come to hustling a fair English rose.

Life is a funny thing, *oui*. One minute you are lock up in jail, the next you are floating in a big Mercedes looking for a stroke.

Some chaps really have it lucky.

But what make life funnier still is that me, Moses, who responsible for the metamorphosis is getting nothing out of the deal, not even a ta for bailing them out, and must needs just stand up there on the pavement while BP step on the x and drive off in his big motor car with brother Galahad.

Bob invite Brenda to come up for a cup of tea. 'Nothing like a strong cup of tea to unwind you after that ordeal,' was the way he put it. Maybe that's how his old lady and old man feel, because whenever he himself was ruffled his thing was to knock back a few strong cups of alcohol.

Anyway, tea it was, to begin with, and while Bob was brewing up Brenda lick her wounds and pour invectives on the Metropolitan Police Force. She say that when they got to the station they were separated, and she did not know what happen to Galahad and BP, but she was stripped and searched, and grilled relentlessly.

'What is it they wanted to find out?' I ask.

'Man,' she say, 'they wanted to find out every goddamn thing you can think of. Who were the dope peddlers in the district; if I did any prostitution; how long BP has been in the country; how often we hold these clandestine meetings; what was the history of the Party, and a host of other irrelevancies. You name it.'

'They must of given a reason for arresting you,' I say reasonably.

'In the end, they said we would be charged with inciting a racial riot. I laugh in their faces.'

Being a loyal subject of Her Majesty, I was still not satisfy that there wasn't a purpose for the swoop.

'What about BP?' I ask. 'Do you think they were after him? Maybe he commit a mayhem in the States and they wanted to extradite him.'

'Yeah, maybe he park the Mercedes on a yellow line,' she sneer.

'Could be', I say.

'Maybe he doesn't have a television licence,' she sneer broader still.

I was so earnest in my quest for justifying the raid that her sarcasm slip me for a moment. 'That's only a minor matter,' I began to object then I realize she was having me on. 'Don't be facetious,' I say coldly. 'It takes two to tango, and I only want to see the other side of the coin.'

'Sometime I wonder if you make all this idle chatter to cover up your brilliance?' she ask innocent now.

'I am not a moron,' I say. 'If I appear persistent to the point of ridicule, it is merely a sign of my honesty. My senses are shocked by tonight's events, and were I assured that the police always behave so irrationally and dictatorial, I would invest my life's saving in the party.'

It was a rash statement, but Brenda really get on my wick, making me feel like a clot. Lucky thing Bob interrupt just then with the tea so she couldn't take me up on it.

'What you think about tonight?' she ask him as he pour her a cup.

Bob, ever willing to knock one, thought she meant what about making beddy-byes together, and he say eagerly, 'Sure, in my room, or you want to go down to the basement?'

Brenda got very angry and jump up. 'What am I doing here in the presence of philistines? One is preoccupied with sex the other is puerile and dotish.'

'You are overwrought,' Bob say. 'You know better than to call me puerile and dotish. You'll feel better after your tea.'

But Brenda flounce out without another word.

▲ ▲ ▲ ▲

It would appear that Fate intervene every time I am in the clear and put me back in a *mooch* and give monkey a go at my pipe. Things was at a stage where I was like a sad billionaire who long for the good old days when he only had a few million or so, for it seem to me that ever since I became a landlord my troubles have multiplied tenfold, and instead of the life of ease and plenty I anticipated, I am beset left right and centre with fresh contention. What touch my soft spot most of all, of course, is that my work was suffering, and it didn't look as if I was writing my Memoirs so much as prognostications and a diary of current events. I longed to get back to my philosophizing and my analysing and my rhapsodizing, decorating my thoughts with little grace-notes and showing the white people that we, too, could write book. But all that come like a dream the way how circumstances continue to pester me and keep me away from my ambition.

The fact that I put up bail for Brenda and Galahad and BP must of sweeten them up and make them believe that I was the blackest philanthropist in Brit'n, for I was hailed and feted, garlanded with pretty flowers like a tourist in Honolulu, and even received a letter from the chairman of the Party, expressing great joy that I had joined the brotherhood in such style as to make up for all my minginess and contrariness in the past, 'and we look forward to a fierce and bloody future with your support.'

But I was keeping a wary eye on these pats on the back. I would gladly have given Bob the honour, for his attitude started to change as rose petals were strewn at my feet.

'What's up with you?' I ask.

'Well you might ask,' he say sulkily. 'Everyone appears to have forgotten that I took a part in all that happened, but you alone get all the glory. I suspect a spot of discrimination.'

'Come come Bob,' I say, 'it's not like you to harbour petty jealousy.'

'I have stood by you through thick and thin,' he say, 'even when it went against the grain. I even supported the movement before you did. And half of that bail money was mine. To what avail?'

'You are acting like a child,' I reprove. 'You know that I don't give one arse for all this laudation.'

'At least they could have mentioned my name in that letter. Perhaps it is because of my colour.'

'Balderdash,' I snort, 'since when does a white man complain of his colour? You should be proud of it, as becomes any staunch Englishman. You want to create a precedence?'

But he was not consoled. 'I am beginning to believe that you black people are planning a great mutiny,' he say. 'It seems I was mistaken in thinking that racial harmony and equality were the Party's objectives.'

'Look Bob,' I say exasperated, 'you want them to strike a medal for you for what you done out of the goodness of your heart?'

I knew that in Bob the Party had a genuine supporter, and it hurt me to hear him express such bitterness. Of more importance, I did not want our personal relationships to be damaged. It is not easy to get a man Friday – even importing au pairs and domestics from the Continent is becoming ticklish, as we in the upper echelons know so well. Bob had served me faithfully, and I wished there was something I could do to mollify his ruffled feelings.

'Listen,' I say, getting an idea, 'you know the Party is bringing out the first issue of their newspaper shortly?'

'I am not interested,' he say listlessly, quaffing his beer.

'How would you like to get your photo on the Front Page?' I ask. It got a lot of white people in this country who live in the abysmal backwoods of society and pine to see their faces in the TV or get their names in the newspapers.

Sure enough he lost his peevishness and perked up at the prospect.

'At least it would be some recognition,' he say. 'It won't satisfy me, but it's better than nothing. Though I doubt you have the influence.'

I had doubts too, so to make sure I went down to the basement right away to see Brenda. It was evening, but she was doing some overtime, preparing copy for the first edition.

'Well Moses,' she say, 'are you enjoying your adulation?'

'That's a lot of shit,' I say. 'Give you-all an inch, and you want a mile.'

'It was Galahad's idea,' she say. 'Left to me, I would not have been so lavish, as I know you still have reservations.'

'All this flattery and praise doesn't go to my head. You should remember Bob instead. His name wasn't even mention once.'

'We're not interested in Bob,' she say. 'However, I am preparing the story of that night and I could bring him in to add colour.' She thought about it, and seem pleased with the idea. 'Yes, it's not a bad idea to use him.'

'A photo on the front page would look good,' I cajole.

'H'mm,' she say.

'Imagine how democratic it would look. The very first issue of a black paper, and a white face dominating the front page. It would put the opposition off their guard.'

'H'mm,' she say. 'Of course, the brutal attack and the arrests is our lead story. I have in mind a full-face picture of a fierce Alsatian.'

'I see your point,' I say. 'Maybe you could have both the Alsatian and Bob?'

'H'mm,' she say, 'h'mm. It's subtle. The subtlety is more likely to be appreciated by a white readership than a black one, though.'

You are the last person I expect to underestimate the intelligence of Our People,' I say.

I could see she was toying with the idea. 'I will put it up to the committee,' she say. 'It has appeal. I suppose you will want credit for it?'

'You can have all the praise,' I say. 'My only motive is to see fair play for Bob. After all, half the bail money was his.'

'We'll see,' she say. 'But while you're here, could you think up a gripping headline?'

'H'mm,' I say, thinking.

'Something that would sell the paper by the headline alone.'

'Alsations Savage Innocent Immigrants?'

'Nothing new in that.'

'Slaughter in North Kensington?'

'Come on, think man.'

'People Panic as Police Pounce?'

She ignore that one.

'How about Brutal Babylon Batter Blacks?'

'Stop making up alliterations. Concentrate on something thoughtful, terse, taut and telling.'

I was beginning to realize what bona fide writers like myself mean when they have to belittle themselves doing hack jobs for the press and TV to pay the mortgage while their magnus opus suffer.

'Listen Brenda,' I say impatiently, 'I can't be bothered with your cheap journalese. I am not that sort of writer, who is only after sensations and scandals. I am writing Literature.'

She burst out in one of those scandalous kya-kya barrack-yard laughs what women from the Caribbean are notorious for. 'You sit down upstairs polishing homilies and belabouring clichés, face-lifting warnout phrases, and you say you are writing

103

literature?'

I stiffened. 'Don't make an ass of yourself,' I say. 'You haven't even seen my manuscript.'

'That's what you think,' she sneer.

'I have it under lock and key, and the key is always in my pocket.' I feel for it and clutch it tightly in my fingers.

'Locks can be picked,' she smirked.

'I believe you are trying to tell me something,' I say uneasily.

'The other day,' she say, 'when you were out, I went upstairs. Bob was there, and I gave him a little bit of crumpet, and afterwards he was like putty in my hands. "Where is this opus I hear Moses is writing?" I ask. "Why do you think of that now?" he asked, feeling for my left tit as he tried to muster his strength for another rounds. "Because I would like to have a look at it," I say. "You'll be lucky," he says, "he keeps it locked up in the cupboard, and keeps the key in his pocket." "Go on, Bob," I say, "you can pick the lock." "I do not want to be disloyal to Moses," he says. "Oh," I say, "in that case you cannot have another go." I would say this much for him, that it was a difficult decision, but he didn't waste much time in jumping out of bed and returning with your precious emmess. And while he was fanning the fire to get his reward, I had a jolly good read.'

I could well imagine the scene, oh yes. I could see that bastard helping Brenda to my drinks, and then taking her to my room, and dirtying up my sheets. I knew he would do anything to get a piece of black pussy, and not for the slightest moment did I entertain any doubt that Brenda spoke the truth. Of all the images that came to my mind, though, the one that was like the last twist of the knife was of her spreadeagled there, chuckling and guffawing over my Memoirs, whilst Bob titillated her to reciprocate to his disgusting lust.

I got up from the chair I was sitting in. 'So!' I cried. 'So!' Bob, like the nobles and statesmen who hold the keys of the kingdom in their hands, had succumbed to the call of the flesh. What a shattering discovery when you put your faith in people, to find that they are only human and err.

'The only sentence you know, Moses,' Brenda went on, delighting in my discomfiture and misery, 'is what criminals get. Your conjunctions and your hyperboles are all mixed up with your syntax, and your figures of speech only fall between 10 and 20. Where you have punctuation you should have allegory and predicates, so that the pronouns appear in the correct context. In other words, you should stick to oral communication and leave the written word to them what knows their business.'

'Say no more!' I cry, covering my ears from the slander and insults. 'Your envy and enmity is not unexpected. The moment a black man lifts his head, his very own kind are the first to drag him down.'

'So you see,' she went on sweetly, 'you are not even capable of thinking up a good headline.'

'How can I think now?' I say, and I was almost in tears, but fighting them back valiantly. 'A masterpiece was coming to me, but your vicious assessment of my work has stultified my brains.'

'Well, think about it when you cool off, after you burn that manuscript. You should be ashamed to be the author of such an ignorant, unschooled piece of work. Really, I thought better of you.'

I left Brenda with a heavy heart. Woe is me. I had barely recovered from Galahad's criticisms when this had to happen. I wince as I thought about it. First he condemn my material, which was one thing, but now Brenda had ridiculed the very foundation and structure, hurling contempt and defamation on my usage of the Queen's language, which had always been my forte, as I have tried to show.

I plod dejectedly up the basement steps, weighed down with the double-barrel barrage she had fire at me. My burden was not only her spitefulness and calcumny which Time would heal – I have been sorely pressed by vicissitudes ere this and am an old hand at turning the other cheek – but there was the crushing blow of Bob's treachery. I don't know which was the harder to bear; I didn't know how to face him, I felt I could never look him in the eye again. I was not angry. I was sad. That's the most hurtful part of it. I couldn't fly into a rage and storm upstairs and accuse him wrathfully for having deceived me. I could only feel melancholia.

And to think that I did went downstairs with good intentions for him!

He was still sitting down, but he had advanced from beer to

whisky on the rocks, and he was looking at some photograph album which he had originally brought with him along with his stock of comic books.

I heaved a great sigh and sit down on the sofa so that I didn't have to face him direct.

'Well?' he rattle the ice in his glass, like a man absorbed drawing attention to his absorbability.

'Brenda thinks it is a good idea,' I manage lifelessly. 'She will put it up to the committee.'

'Good show. I was just scanning some photographs that I have,' he say, probably scanning them all over again, lifting them up to the light and squinting, 'but none of them do me justice.'

'Justice!' I spat out the word. 'It got no justice. They say the world is round, but a donkey shit square.'

He was too engrossed in looking at his own physiognomy to listen. 'What do you think of this one?' he shove the album at me.

'It's okay,' I say, without looking.

'It's old, though. I took it out years ago. You think the Party has enough funds to send a photographer around to snap me?'

'Don't ask me no bloody thing,' I say, getting even more irritable that he couldn't notice the mood I was in.

'I shouldn't have to give them a picture, anyway, they must have a cameraman if they're running a newspaper. You never saw this album before, have you?'

'How could I?' I began listlessly, but gathered tone. 'You never showed it to me. And I honour your privacy, you know. I don't go prying into your things, unlike some people I know. One in particular.'

'It reminds me of my life up north, before I came to London.' I might as well of not spoken. He was holding the album close to me, thinking that I was watching as he slowly turn the pages. He laugh and give me a dig with his elbow. 'Look at this family group. That's Mum and Dad at the back, and me and my two brothers and sister in the front. My sister got married to a Welshman who gives her a hard time. They have two children. I've got a picture of them together somewhere,' and he turn the page. 'Ah, here. I took this one out myself.'

'It's time you paid them a visit, isn't it? Why don't you pack up and return to the Black Country?' Once again I threw all the sarcasm and bitterness I could into my tone, but it was lost. It look as if as far as I concern it's easy to take insults, but an art I don't know is to insult other people, apparently.

Bob laugh wistfully. 'Maybe I will. I haven't seen them for years. And my holidays are due.'

'The time's ripe now,' I say. 'Might as well enjoy all that blood money you got from hoarding them Pakis.'

'Yeah.'

'When you think of going, that's the time to go. Maybe you'll like it up there and stay,' I add hopefully.

'Perhaps after my picture appears in the newspapers,' he say, 'It'll be something to talk about. Look at this one of me with a tart from my home town.'

'You could visit her too,' I say without looking.

The wistful note crept back into his voice. 'Man, she was hard to lay, you know? I had to spend a lot of money before I got her in the mood. But it was worth it. Yes siree.' And he laugh reminiscently.

'You'd do anything for a bit of pussy, won't you?' I say bitterly, 'even deceive your friends?'

It was coming out, I had it all pent-up, and I suppose I couldn't hold it back any longer.

'Eh?' he say. 'What's that?'

'You know bloody well what I mean,' I say, warming now. 'You would sneak and beg and crawl and creep. Nothing is below you to get a bird beneath you. Like Brenda for instance.'

'I had Brenda many times,' he brag.

'I refer to one particular night. When you picked the lock and showed her my Memoirs, even though you know how sensitive I am about it.'

He look up from the photograph album for the first time. But he didn't have the guts to look me in the eye. He just lift his head and glance around the penthouse, giving himself time to think, to fabricate some hollow excuse for his despicable behaviour.

'She told you?' he say.

'Truth will out,' I say, and I taunted him. 'Go on, make your feeble excuses, as I know you will.'

'You know how it is when you are in heat, Moses,' he put down the album and pick up his whisky. His hand was shaking. 'I did

107

not stop to think.'

'No doubt you must have read it time and again yourself,' I say with such rancour as I could manage in my wretchedness. 'Have you no caustic comment to make about the juxtaposition of my adjectives?'

'I never read a word. I swear that.'

'Bah!' I spat. 'Don't add hypocrisy to your sins, spare me your lies, at least own up like a man and stand the bounce.'

'I tell you, Moses, I have never set eyes on it, knowing how delicate your feelings are.'

I gagged. I almost puked. In my disconcernment I snatched his glass and had a swig of whisky, the first time strong drink ever passed my lips. When I was a little boy in Trinidad my mother had to *force* a little brandy pass my throat when I had a fresh-cold – to kill the germs, she said.

'The damage it done,' I say quietly. 'What's the use of talking?'

'I've done worse things and you never reacted like this,' he rebuke.

'You won't understand,' I say. 'What do you know of the deep maelstroms churning inside an author, or how *touchous* he could be concerning his work?'

'I can see that's one fuck I'll live to regret,' Bob say thoughtfully.

'Aye,' I say, 'right on. Swinging. You may consider the incident forgotten, but not forgiven. I still await a formal apology.'

'Don't be so bloody fussy,' he say, 'I've as much as said I'm sorry.'

'You haven't couched it in the proper words or manner,' I say stubbornly. Maybe I was pushing it too far, but I could still feel a nasty taste in my mouth from Brenda's virulence.

Bob capsize his drink and finish it, and get up. 'I'm going to bed. We'll talk tomorrow, when you are in a better mood.'

I didn't say anything, just let him go, leaving his photograph album on the table. I don't know how long I sat there after he left, calming myself thinking of sandy beaches and waving coconut palms in my beloved homeland, remembering little joys and pleasures to soothe my mind. Familiarity breeds contempt, and the thought was coming to me that Bob should really have a vacation, and get out of my sight and hearing until such time as I convalesced.

I took up the photograph album and began to look at the pictures randomly. Some of them was loose, and as I turn the one what had him and that blowsy wench, I notice an address on the back: JEANNIE DANIELS, CHEZ NOUS, MOSCOW AVENUE, ASHBY-DE-LA-ZOUCH, LEICESTERSHIRE. And underneath that, these words: COME BACK TO JEANNIE, BOBBIE!

I sit down at the table and write a letter: Dear Jeannie, I hope you will not think me presumptious, but I got your address from a photograph which Bobbie keeps in his wallet (close to his heart) during the day, and under his pillow at night. Bobbie has been staying with me since he came to London, and I cannot tell you how much he misses you, and calls your name day and night. I don't know how he bears being separated from you for such a long time. He has been working so hard that he is on the verge of a nervous breakdown, and is really in need of a break to get away from the hurly-burly polluted atmosphere of London. He has told me of those pleasant walks together with you down an English lane gathering lilacs, and I feel a change of air would do him a world of good, and being with you would be a tonic in itself. I am taking it upon myself to write this letter as a surprise for him, hoping that you will invite him to come and visit you. You can reply to this address because, as I say, he is here with me, and he is really in bad shape.

Nothing venture nothing gain. Two days after I post the letter a reply come for Bob. I steam it open: Dearest Bobbie! You promised to write when you went to London but I never heard a word from you. It is only through the kindnest of your friend that I got the address. My darling I miss you from the day you left. You must come right away before you get any worst in London, and we will have some good times like we did. I am writing immideatly so that you can come from this very weekend, because Mum is going away for a few weeks (to her sister in Scotland) and we will be by our selves. Don't get too many ideas, though. I close with all my love for you alone, Bobbie, XXX, Jeannie. (PS Can you bring me a bra, cup C, and a few pairs of nylons, as I cannot get good ones here, and leave it up to you to decide what colour.)

I gloated over the success of my enterprise by having a scotch on the rocks. (It just goes to show you how you go downhill once you get started on the Demon drink.) When Bob come home I had one waiting for him too.

'What's this,' he say, 'you've come to your senses?'

I hadn't said a word to him since that night.

'There's a letter for you,' I say.

'For me?' he look astounded.

'Yes.'

'Oh. See what it is,' he say, and move to the sideboard to put more ice in his drink.

I read the letter loud, and he stay right over there listening, as if the acoustics was better there. When I finish I explain what I had done.

'I hope you're not annoyed,' I say. 'It's just that you seem homesick and sentimental the other night, and I acted on the spur of the moment.'

'I'm tempted,' he say musingly, 'but can you manage on your own?'

I wave my hand in the air. 'It won't be easy. But I'll get Brenda to come up and lend a hand when she could.'

'Jeannie,' he say softly.

'With the light brown hair,' I egg, singing the line.

'Pity we can't both go,' he say.

'One of us has got to hold the fort,' I say.

'I'll try to be gone only for a week or two,' he say.

'Don't hurry back,' I say. 'Stay as long as you like. In fact, the way things are going here, it won't surprise me if you decide you are better off in the Black Country.'

'You're not trying to get rid of me, are you,' he say with a twinkle in his eye.

'God forbid,' I say, 'but I don't want to stand in your way. There doesn't appear to be any future for you in London. How will you travel, by coach or train?'

'I may fly,' he said, 'and land up there in style. Jeannie is impressed by little things like that.'

'Have a good time,' I say, 'and don't worry about me, I'll be all right.'

The better part of the Friday night he spend hoovering, spitting and polishing the penthouse until it got on my nerves.

'That'll do Bob, you don't want to tire yourself out for Jeannie.'

'You sure you'll be okay on your own? You know where everything is?'

'Yeah, yeah. Go to bed, you have an early flight in the morning.'

So he left the Saturday, taking a suitcase with some clothes, and a stock of comic books to browse on the flight.

▲ ▲ ▲ ▲

A peace descend on the penthouse after Bob gone. In the lull, I congratulated myself for getting rid of him. At last I had a chance to size up the way things was going, to recover my equilibrium and equanimity. I started to make plans about the house. I thought of selling up and retreating to Cornwall or the Chilterns. I did tell Bob that he had no future in London, but what the arse had I? Who would buy a house with a short lease that the LCC was going to knock down soon? Then I thought of Brenda and her insults, and Galahad and Black Power, and the pending trial, and how I was so stupid to put up bail for them. I tried to work on the book, but when I sit down to write, all these depressing thoughts keep humbugging me. I start to take a closer look at my phraseology and my spelling, and if I could find any grammatical errors or incorrect punctuations, but I didn't see any, it look just as good as anything Shakespeare or Billy Wordsworth ever write; that black bitch Brenda was only green with envy, not even a comma or a common noun was askew.

In the midst of all these afflicted thoughts, the door knock and Paki come in. The very sight of him on top of everything else was enough to make me choke.

'What the arse you want,' I snarl.

'There's some trouble,' he say.

I shuddered. 'Please,' I plead.

'Nothing to do with immigrants,' he say quickly. 'It's something personal.'

'Even so,' I begged.

111

'It's my wives in Southall,' he say. 'I want one of them to come and live with me.'

'You'd better see Bob about these domestic details,' I say.

'I haven't seen him around.'

'He's on long vacation.'

'When is he coming back?'

'I don't know. Don't bother me.'

'This is urgent. My wives don't get on with each other, and Fatima is threatening to leave the harem unless I get her away.'

'Wait a minute,' I say. 'How come you live here if you've got wives in Southall?'

'They think I am in Pakistan.'

'I retract that question,' I say swiftly, I don't want to hear another word.'

'Then it's okay for Fatima to come?'

'Yeah, yeah, don't bother me.' I wasn't going to get involved in all that shit again, especially when I was feeling moody.

'What about the rent?'

'Discuss all that with Bob when he returns. Please leave, Paki.'

'There is no god but *the* god,' he began.

'Get lost,' I interrupt.

'I just wanted to say that there's a queue of tenants waiting outside.'

'What for?'

He shrug. 'Bob's away, I guess you'll have to take his place.'

He barely went out of the door before Flo, the Barbados woman come in. Like with Galahad, there was no preliminary, only aggression.

'Way Bob?' she demanded.

'He's away,' I say.

'He promise to fix the bloody ascot in my room. I pays a high rent and the least you can do is give me some hot water.'

'I'll have it attended to.'

'When? More than a week now and it ain't working.'

'Tomorrow. I'll get the plumber in.'

'You better. I been thinking of going to the Rent Tribunal, you know. That high rent and no blooming hot water.'

'Tomorrow, Flo. Please. My nerves are frayed.'

'Maybe you should of gone on holiday instead of him.'

112

'Tomorrow, Flo. Tomorrow-please-God.'

'I hope so,' she says as she go.

'Next!' I called, thinking I might as well get into the fun of the thing before worry kill me.

Ojo, the African, come in in his conductor uniform. as if he just hop off his bus.

'Hello bo, how you go, oh?' he say.

'I go so-so, bo,' I say. 'How you go, Ojo?'

'I do not see much of you, Mr Moses.'

'I'm busy. What do you want?'

'I look for Bob many days now.'

'He's away. On holiday.'

'Oh. So.' He study that. 'He owe me some change.'

'How much?'

'Two pounds.'

I gave him the money. 'Send in the next one, will you,' I say.

Alfonso, the Cypriot, come.

'When's Bob coming back home?' he query.

'I'm not sure. What's wrong?'

'I wanted to see him on a personal matter.' He start to leave then turn back. 'I got rats in my room. You better get rid of them before they spread.'

Macpherson, the Australian followed.

'What can I do for you, cobber?' I ask.

'Did Bob leave a parcel for me?'

'No.'

'That's funny. He promised to. Maybe it's in his room?'

'I'll have a look later.'

'I'm going out now. If you find it, keep it for me, will you?'

'Okay.'

When he left I open a can of beer with trembling hands. My nerves were screaming, I hear a step and without turning say, 'What can I do for you?'

'You having problems with your tenants?' Galahad come in.

When I see him the beer was foaming out of the can, and I, too, was almost foaming at the mouth. I burst into a kind of manic laughter, a wild riotous mirth that overspilled out of me so that I shook, shaking the can, and the beer and I bubble over.

'Galahad,' I gasp, barely able to control myself – but some

113

innate sense of preservation making my thumb plug the hole in the can – 'Galahad, please tell me the world is coming to an end, that the house is on fire, and that I have two seconds to live.'

'Nothing fortuitous as all that,' he say, 'but grave enough. BP has absconded.'

'He won't be here for the trial?'

'It isn't only that. He has absconded with the Party's funds.'

'Come now.' I tried to sound natural, but the words came out in a hoarse, throaty whisper. 'This isn't a music-hall farce, man, or a television comedy.'

'If I lie I die,' Galahad say. 'Where's Bob. I'd like him to fetch me a beer.'

'You'll have to get it yourself, I'm afraid. Bob's away.'

He went out to the fridge in the kitchen.

Strange, I mused, I feel as if I could cope with the Spanish Armada or the Boston Tea Party, but a simple thing like Galahad's disclosure make me feel incapacitated. I tried to put everything in perspective and pull myself together. Perhaps we can all manage our affairs reasonably well if adversities came in some regulated order, so that we could deal with them one by one. One might even disciple the days and have it all tidy: Monday – Income Tax; Tuesday – Galahad; Wednesday – Brenda; Thursday – Paki; Friday – Income Tax; Saturday – Bob; Sunday – Black Power. It's a short week, but what can you do? It's when there is a spate of adverse events that we weaken, and the continuous battering at your senses make you come like a punch-drunk boxer who can't even raise his gloves to ward off his opponent. But there is a further stage even, when, like in drunkenness, your defensive mechanism takes an enforced respite, and you get that feeling of euphoria, and ready to laugh kiff-kiff at anything, even the news that a crash is imminent and you should fasten your seat-belt.

'Give me the ballad,' I say merrily, relaxing on the sofa as Galahad come back. 'Spare me no gruesome detail.'

'What can I say?' Galahad shrug. He was worried too, but he wasn't even miles near my stage. 'We trusted BP – you saw and heard for yourself. He has just disappeared off the scene.'

'How did he get at the Party's coffers?' I chuckle.

'A simple matter for a man of his importance in the black

114

world. We don't know all the details yet, but it seems he wanted to examine the books. And of course we can't allow the police to investigate.'

'How much did he get away with?' I was really relaxed and enjoying all this.

'About five hundred pounds. There isn't a half-pee left in the kitty. However, we may be able to pass the hat' – here he give me a wink, but I didn't bat an eye; I might of been in euphoria but my feet were on the ground – 'and that's only a material loss. It is the theft itself by a trusted brother that is the shattering blow. It might have grave repercussions throughout the Third World. We are trying to hush up the whole sordid affair. You got any whisky to chase this beer?'

'Why not?' I say headily, waving to the decanter and glasses on the dumbwaiter. 'I'm sorry Bob isn't here to serve you – you can pour some for me too.'

'Where is he, out chasing pussy?'

'Yeah, up in Leicestershire.'

Galahad whistle. 'He must have a great thirst.'

'He's gone to look up old friends. I hope the bastard doesn't return.'

'Go on, what'll you do without your Man Friday? By the way, we've decided to use his picture in the paper.'

'Oh? In view of developments I thought all Party plans would be held in abeyance?'

'We can't allow ourselves to stagnate. We've had drawbacks before. I don't know what's going to happen about the case, though.' He rattle the ice in his whisky, just like Bob. 'We were expecting an impassioned oration from BP in the courtroom. Now it's all left to me.'

'What about Madame Brenda?' I sneer. 'She is full of eloquence and presumes a superlative knowledge of language.'

'Of course. A woman will invoke great public sympathy. Is Bob any good at addressing a crowd?'

'Why worry if nothing's decided,' I say easily. 'You're only extending your troubles unduly.'

'We've got to be prepared, anyway. When is he coming back? I'll have to brief him. Evidence from a white man will carry enormous weight.'

115

I was beginning to feel a reaction to my euphoria, getting fed up with every bloody thing. In this life you barely happy for a minute, even if it's false, before the apple cart get upset.

'You look tired,' Galahad say.

'Who, me? I'm as fresh as a daisy.'

'I don't suppose I could stay the night,' he say, as if to himself, 'I could sleep in Bob's room.'

I left it like that without replying; the very thought of his presence in the house would depress me further.

'Anyway,' he went on, 'I was only testing you. I do not have to catch any lousy bus. BP left the Mercedes behind. Every cloud has a silver lining.' He sigh at my continued silence. 'I don't know what's coming over you, Moses. You are really going round the bend.'

'Yeah,' I say, 'and you're pushing.'

'I've always been your friend. I hate to see you go to pieces this way.'

'Not to worry. I will remember you in my will.'

'At the rate you're going, better hurry and draw it up,' he fire this pleasantry at me as a parting shot before he departed.

Left alone, I sunk into even lower spirits. I pondered this new blow to my Memoirs. I refer to BP's last exit to Brooklyn, for I had an eye on the possibilities of selling my American rights. Without a Yank at Oxford my goose was cook. Look how, in all them television scripts, the writers *bound* to have an American character, no matter how incongruous he fit, otherwise the US mongols blow cigar smoke in your face when you try to peddle your work in the States. As you know, I didn't have to dream up BP or invent him, he just naturally appear on the scene of his own accord and bam! before I could get a chance to exploit him as a character, he ups and clear off, leaving me high and dry. What did I have to comfort me? Whose shoulder was available to cry on? I thought of phoning the Good Samaritans and having a heart-to-heart chat; I even thought of dialling nine nine nine and ask them to send the booby wagon. And then, I tried to pull myself together. There must be other people in this world worse off than me. Think of Oxfam, Moses, I told myself, think of Dr Barnardo's Home and the Benevolent Fund for those in show business who can no longer bring a smile to our lips nor earn them millions of pounds no more; think of the blind and the maimed, the destitute and the desolate, the wretched hippies and drop-outs spending their lives at the foot of little Eros in Piccadilly Circus. A tear came to my eye as I thought of Les Miserables, and the water cleared my vision so I saw how selfish I was, wallowing in self-pity instead of commiserating with those who really know the tragedy of total misery. And not only sympathizing, but trying to do something practical to better their lot. What pleasure was I getting out of my landlordship or out of the blood money earned from the traffic of illegal immigrants? Where was the high life and the champagne and the invitation to the Garden Party in Buckingham Palace, driving up in my Rolls with the number plate BLACK 1, and batman Bob chauffering? And even if all of these things were added onto me, what were they but evanescent, hollow delights that could never still the poignant pangs of conscience? I flagellated myself. I thought how I had just turned a countryman out in the cold night. I thought how I did connive to get rid of my best white friend Bob (and what for, but vanity?) whose absence I was already ruing. I thought with what *grudgedity* I did pay bail for Galahad and Brenda and BP when they was trying to help my Own People, and how tightfisted I had become. I thought of all those poor orientals who would become an added burden on the innocent British taxpayer purely because of my selfishness.

I suppose, really, this is what is meant when one sees the light, like how Saul become Paul. I try out Moses – Roses, and it come to me in a flash, like a revelation.

Without further ado, dear R, let me say that after these sober reflections, I resolve to turn over a new leaf.

▲ ▲ ▲ ▲

Now, as the days went by, I missed Bob more and more, but I busy myself attending to the needs of my tenants, so that things would be shipshape when he come back. I *did* stop to think, as I was putting rat poison in the Cypriot room and bounce my head hard under the mantelpiece, that in fact Crusoe was swapping roles with Friday, but it didn't weaken my new resolution. Rather strengthen it, for humility is a virtue too few of we have.

In these domestic chores Brenda lend me a generous hand, going down on she hands and knees to scrub the floor, and spending all her spare time dashing about the house. I stilled thoughts of ulterior motives.

Bob telephone after a fortnight of freedom. He sound chirpy. I was glad to hear his voice. Honest.

'Moses! How are things in London?'

'Fine. How are things in Ashby-de-la-Zouch.'

'Groovy man. Swinging.'

'You'd better hurry back. The Party photographer wants to take your picture for the paper.'

'I've been thinking about that. I'm returning tomorrow evening.'

'That's cool.'

'I'm bringing Jeannie with me. She's never been to London before.'

'That's cool too.'

Jeannie must of been in the telephone booth with him for I hear him make an aside.

'Oh.' He sound disappointed at my ready reply. 'I expected you to raise objections?'

'Come off it. Your friends are my friends.'

'You sound a lot better than when I left,' he say uneasily. 'You haven't got another fag in, have you?'

'Tommyrot. It's just that I've been thinking things over. You'll find me a different man.'

I could envisage him puzzling over my warm-heartedness, not knowing what to say.

'Well, we'll see you tomorrow then.'

'Right on. Give Jeannie my love.'

'Will do.'

I went into the kitchen where Brenda was preparing *côtelettes de veau papillotes* for our supper.

'Bob's coming back tomorrow,' I say gaily.

'Good show,' she say. 'I'll get the photographer to come around.'

'He's bringing Jeannie with him.'

'Who's she?'

'Oh, some bluefoot tart he's hooked with.'

118

'I'll clean up his room after we've had supper.'

'Yes,' I say, then thoughtful, 'Do you think I ought to put a double bed in his room?'

'He and me manage okay on the one he has,' she say.

'That's you,' I say, 'but we don't want to give Jeannie the wrong impression on her first visit to the city.'

Brenda snort. 'Or is it because she's white?'

'You berate me when I have bad intentions,' I say. 'now you berate me when I have good ones. Please don't. I won't have anything left.'

'Okay,' Brenda say. 'You're too useful to make an enemy of.'

'It's just that I dig Bob,' I say. 'Perhaps we can spring a little surprise party for them?' It sounded like gilding the lily, but what the hell. Man cannot live by bread along. 'Nothing elaborate. A case of champagne, and some snacks like Dublin prawns and smoked salmon. You could bring up your record player and we'll have some music.'

'H'mm,' Brenda say. I could see she was warming to the idea. Nothing like a freeness to get black people to shake off dull sloth. 'I'll do the snacks,' she offer. 'How about invitees?'

'I don't know any of Bob's friends,' I say, a little surprised at the fact. 'I suppose we could have Galahad, and Paki, if you stretch the meaning of friendship. It doesn't sound crowdish enough to polish off a case of bubbly, though.'

'Bob's got lots of friends,' Brenda say. 'Leave everything to me. We will have a ball.'

'Why not?' I say recklessly. 'I didn't even give a house-warming when I acquired the property. It's time I let my hair down a little and have some fun.'

The next day I went to a record shop and buy *Jeannie With The Light Brown Hair*, which I thought I would put on first when the party start, as a sort of welcoming gesture. I try to get the double bed but the store say they can't deliver before 1984, and my lease would expire before that.

Brenda went to town on the penthouse and put up balloons and chinese lanterns and other decorations, and she brought up some Black Power propaganda from the basement and tack them about on the walls with drawing pins. I was a little dubious about this, but she was doing all the work so I keep quiet. I open a

119

bottle of champagne and she and me had a few drinks, so that by the time guests start to arrive we was both a little high.

I did not know that Bob had so many black friends. They trickled in, but little drops of water make the mighty ocean, and before long the room was full up. Bob and Jeannie didn't turn up yet and I was getting a little anxious, as black people do not dilly-dally when they are at a party, and already raggae music was blasting, and they had started an incursion into the case of champagne.

I haul Brenda aside from amidst a group of agitators who was rapping loudly about the future of the Party.

'I didn't know Bob had so many dark friends,' I say.

'What's the matter?' she sneer. 'Changed your mind already about your good intentions?'

'It's not that,' I say. 'But this is a rather riff-raff lot. Couldn't you of asked Lamming and Salkey and some of their English contemporaries?'

'All these people here have paid to come in,' Brenda say.

'You've stolen my thunder,' I accuse. 'I wanted to give them a freeness.'

'You are,' she say. 'You're not getting anything out of it. The takings will go to swell the Party's swindled funds.'

I went over to Paki who was sitting with a small harem of three, dressed in their national costume. He was drinking, but the women was silent and just looking on with expressionless miens.

'Hello,' I say. 'which one is Fatima?'

He nod his head at a buxom one.

'Are they all living here with you?' I ask.

'No,' he say, 'they take turns.'

'There is no god but Allah,' I say, riding my champagne wave, refusing to allow any alarming thoughts to spoil my evening.

'And Mohammed is his prophet,' Paki agree. 'You should bring the drinks out of the kitchen so we can help ourselves.'

I mingled with my guests. The crowd was so thick that I spill champagne against a gentleman's jacket who was dancing.

'I'm so sorry,' I say.

He look at me coldly. 'Did you pay to get in?' he say.

'I am the host,' I say stiffly.

'Oh. I thought you was a gate-crasher. There's a few here.'

120

I shrugged and moved to Galahad, escorting a Bayswater blonde. (Like how an intrepid mountaineer still have a safety rope lest he bust his arse scaling the heights, so those who cry Black Power loudest usually have a white woman in tow, whether as lifeline or whipping-boy I leave to you.)

'What's the time, Galahad?' I ask. 'Bob should be here by now?'

He glance at his watch. 'You know what transport is like these days. If I knew I'd have met them at the station in the Mercedes.'

'Yeah.'

'Say, that chap in the corner with them fancy birds – is that Faizull?'

'No, it's Paki.'

'H'mm. You think he'll know if that caretaker's job in the country is still vacant?'

'Why don't you ask him?'

'Does he understand English?'

'Better than you and me.'

'Good. I'll have chat with him later.' Galahad grin. 'No harm in having a second string to my bow, the cost of living being what it is.'

Brenda come up to us. 'Bob's arrived,' she say. 'He's coming up the stairs now.'

'Quick!' I cried. 'Take off that raggae and put on Jeannie With The Light Brown Hair.'

'Why don't you get everybody to sing For He's a Jolly Good Fellow,' she sneer.

I didn't wait but went to the record player myself and take off the raggae. Everybody who was dancing start to boo but I didn't mind them. I put on my greetings record, and as Bob and Jeannie come in, the strains of *J W T L B H* filled the room, played by the London Philharmonic Symphony Orchestra, in your rarse!

'What's going on?' Bobbie ask, bemused, as I meet him at the door.

'Just a little welcoming party for you and Jeannie,' I say.

'Damned white of you, old boy.'

'Don't mention it,' I blush pink, but neither of them notice.

'Allow me to introduce Moses,' Bobbie say to Jeannie. 'He's our landlord.'

'Come come,' I say. 'Don't be so formal. I'm more of a friend.' Jeannie shake hands.

You might of noticed that I have been refraining from too much descriptive prose, but you might forgive me if I say briefly that if Ashby-de-la-Zouch produce such fair creatures, I would turn my back on Londontown like Dick Whittington and head for them thar parts as straight as the crow flies – and I am not inexperienced in these assessments, as you have no doubt gathered.

'Jeannie,' I say, gushing. 'Well come and welcome. Make yourself completely at home. What I have is yours.'

'How gallant,' she give me a coy smile; if she had a fan she would of hide her face behind it. I thought if I did make a prettier speech I might of got more than a smile. But there was no hurry.

'Hark to the music,' I say. 'It is especially for you.'

'What is it?' she ask, harking.

But at the same moment, some bloody cunt went and put back on the raggae record.

'Never mind,' I say, 'we will listen to it together another day when it is not so noisy and crowded.'

Galahad and Brenda come up and get introduce; Brenda bring them champagne. I could see that cattish look in Brenda eye.

'What's that place you're from, Irma de la Douce?' she ask Jeannie sweetly.

'Brenda is a bit of a wit,' I laugh it off. 'Show Jeannie where she can powder her nose, dear.'

Bobbie and me left them and went into the kitchen. Bobbie start to take off his jacket.

'What's the matter, you hot?' I ask.

'No. But there are all these guests to be attended to. I wish you'd told me, I would have caught an earlier train.' And he start to distribute patties in the paper plates.

'Leave all that, man,' I protest, 'you have the night off. It's your party.'

'You're sure?'

'Yes. Brenda and her helpers will do all that.'

'Okay.' He relax. 'What's new, then?'

'I am,' I say, and I tell him how I did see the light after some lucubrations, and that henceforth I would try to do good unto others rather than think of myself alone.

Instead of applauding my conversation Bobbie get vex. 'I only leave you alone for a couple of weeks and you become completely disorganized,' he say. 'You're even drinking champagne.'

'I've made up my mind,' I say stubbornly. 'Let's eat, drink, and be merry. You have cause for celebration.'

'What cause?' he argue. 'We had a good relationship before.'

'But not on equal terms. From now on we live like friends, not master and servant.'

'You mean I'll have to start paying rent, don't you?' he ask suspiciously, looking my gift horse in the mouth.

Alas, that men always think the worst of their fellows. 'Don't be an ingrate,' I say. 'It isn't going to cost you anything. Consider it as reward for good service, if you like. Come, let's change the subject.'

But it was Brenda who change it, coming into the kitchen. 'The photographer is here for Bobbie,' she announce.

That perked him up. 'Good,' he say.

'Better bring him in here, away from that crowd,' I say.

Bobbie put back on his jacket and take a comb from his pocket and pass it through his hair. He rub his fingers on the edges of his teeth like Burt Lancaster when he looking in the mirror.

The photographer come with a big camera strap around his shoulders like a American tourist.

'Where's Jeannie?' Bobbie ask Brenda.

'She's still in the loo,' Brenda say.

'I'd like her to see this,' Bobbie say.

'Oh come on,' Brenda say impatiently, 'we haven't got all day.' She put him to sit down on the kitchen stool, twisting his head this way and that like she was going to give him a trim.

Whilst this was going on I went to look for Jeannie. As I pass the toilet I hear a banging and when I look I see where Brenda bolt the door from the outside. I opened it and rescued Jeannie.

'Where's Bobbie?' she ask, recovering her composure.

'He's being photographed,' I say, 'Shall we dance?'

We squeezed on to the floor, barely able to move, which I thought was all the better as Jeannie had to jam up against me as we dance. I would of like to whisper sweet nothings in her ear, but the bloody music was playing so loud. In fact, as the night progress it become louder, as if to match the height of pleasure which I was proudly responsible for for all these people. But pride goeth before a fall.

We were felled by two officers of the law. Brenda came to tell me, seething.

'Bleeding Babylon,' she snarl. 'Not unexpected, but certainly unwelcomed. Better go and talk to them. I will get the photographer to take some shots.'

I went to the door.

Break it up,' the senior say without preliminary. 'Too much noise.'

'This is a private party, officer,' I say.

'Break it up.' It didn't sound as if he hear me. He peep over my shoulder as if he and his mate want to implement the order themselves, but change his mind when he see the mob behind me.

'Just break it up,' he say for the third time, 'or there'll be trouble,' and they start to go without another word.

A primitive went and turn up the volume louder.

'We got a couple of shots,' Brenda say with satisfaction. 'Now we'll just stick around and wait for them to return with reinforcements. It will make good copy for the paper.'

'No,' I say firmly. 'Enough's enough. It was good while it lasted.'

But Sister Brenda had her hackles up. 'If you want us to leave, we'll continue in the basement,' and she begin to direct the traffic downstairs, and take up the record player and records and went.

Suddenly the penthouse was quiet. Not back to normal by any means with the debris left behind ('I will take care of all that,' Bobbie tell Brenda before she left) but only Bobbie and Jeannie and me remain.

'Tired?' I ask her.

'Yes,' she say, 'it was a nice party, though.'

The three of we was sitting on the sofa, but Bobbie had himself between she and me, as if to stake his claim from the beginning.

'Shall we tell him?'Bobbie ask Jeannie.

She giggle. 'If you like.'

124

'Jeannie and I are getting married,' Bobbie say.

'Sure,' I say, waving it away. I always used to tell everybody, when they see me with a bird, that we going to get married. It not only clear up misunderstanding, but it suppose to keep marauders away, like a chastity belt. Also, I didn't put it past Bobbie to make rash promises in order to get Jeannie into his clutches – I done the same many times. I decide the friendly thing would be to augment his honourable intentions.

'Bobbie spoke of you constantly,' I say, 'I feel as if we were old friends. I hope you like it here.'

She giggle again. 'Depends on Bobbie,' she say.

'Don't you believe me?' Bobbie ask me.

'Sure, sure,' I say.

'Show him the ring,' Bobbie say, taking her hand and performing the action himself. 'What d'you think of that?'

It was a cheap sparkler from Woolworths but I say loyally, 'That must of set you back a few quid.'

'It's real diamonds,' Jeannie say, as if she expected a more awesome reaction.

'I have no doubt,' I say. 'Bobbie would get you nothing but the best. He's that sort of fellow.'

'Does it convince you?' Bobbie ask.

I wanted to say that Jeannie was the one he had to convince, but I say, 'Yes. Now I see you are in deadly earnest. Congratulations.'

'I want you to know, so you wouldn't get any wrong ideas.'

And Jeannie come up with, 'I'm not that kind of girl.'

'Now that we've cleared that up,' I say, 'is there anything left to eat? I'm famished.'

Habits die hard. Bobbie leapt to his feet. 'I'll get you something,' he say.

'Sit down with your fiancée,' I say. 'I'll get it myself.'

I went into the kitchen. I was feeling mellow, in spite of the fuzz. It had been a nice party, and it was good to rub shoulders with My People, who had all behaved with the greatest circumspect. And having Jeannie with us was filled with pregnancy, in a manner of speaking.

It was an auspicious start to my new philanthropy. I feel like a boy scout who done his good turn for the day.

▲ ▲ ▲ ▲

The very next morning Bobbie say he was going to the Registry
for them to put up the banns.

'You don't have to carry on the charade with me, old thing. I
understand,' I say.

'You find it incomprehensible that I am marrying Jeannie?' he
raised his eyebrows. 'You have made certain adjustments to your
way of life. During the holiday I made some decisions too.'

'Oh come off it,' I scoff. 'What d'you want to get married for?
Is Jeannie on the way?'

'No.'

'What's the panic then?'

'I want to get it over and done with.'

'Marriage carries grave responsibilities,' I wag a finger at him
jovially.

'You're wasting your breath this time, Moses.'

'Look,' I say, 'if you are scared that I fancy Jeannie, you're
right. But you do not have to take such drastic measures. I am not
a sex maniac. We could come to some gentleman's agreement,
like we did with Brenda.'

'Don't drag Jeannie down to your level,' he cried heatedly. 'I
am telling you we're getting married.'

It look as if he was serious in truth. 'This is sudden, isn't it?'

'Maybe for you. We've known each other a long time.'

I could not stand aside and watch my friend put his head in the
noose without some show of remonstration, even if he was white.

'Look Bobbie,' I say, 'do you realize what you are putting
yourself in for? Be sensible, old bean.'

'I would like you to be best man,' he say.

'Oh well.' I shrug. You can lead a horse to the water, but you
cannot make him drink. 'It's your funeral.'

Thus did Bobbie entrap himself and decide to tie the nuptial
knot around his own neck, in spite of all the well-meaning advice
I could give him.

A couple of days later, while the banns was up, Brenda come
upstairs with a proof copy of the front page hot off the press.

'There you are Bobbie,' she say, throwing it at him.

He was looking at a comic at the time whilst me and Jeannie was watching television. I switch off the set and all of us crowd round the table, looking down at the front page. POLICE RAID INNOCENT BLACK MEETING, the headline went.

I glanced at Brenda. 'That's pretty tame, isn't it?'

'It's what the editorial board selected,' she say.

It had a three-column picture of an Alsatian dog baring its teeth in a nasty snarl at Bobbie, who was in a half-column picture at the side.

'I don't like it,' Jeannie say.

'Don't like what?' Brenda ask coldly.

'That picture of my Bobbie. It doesn't look like him.'

'You mean you don't like it appearing in a black paper, don't you?' Brenda taunt.

'Pack it up girls,' I say.

'Can I have a dozen copies?' Bobbie ask.

'What for?' Jeannie ask. 'You're not sending that horrible thing to Ashby-de-la-Zouch, are you?'

'And why not pray?' Brenda answer for him. 'It will educate those country bumpkins who think all's quiet on the western front.'

'I thought I could just tear out the front pages and send those,' Bobbie tell Jeannie.

'It's an awful picture, Bobbie.' Jeannie was close to tears.

'What d'you expect, Marlon Brando?' Brenda sneer. 'Take a good look at your dear Bobbie.'

'Let's be amicable,' I say. 'Look at all the wide publicity Bobbie will get for his part in the affair.'

'You should never have got mixed up with those blacks,' Jeannie was crying for real now.

'Just as I always thought,' Brenda sniff. 'She's colour-prejudiced.'

'I'm not!' Jeannie say. 'I like Moses, don't I?'

'There there,' I say, 'don't distress yourself.'

'Leave Jeannie alone Brenda,' Bobbie say. 'Don't forget we're going to be married soon.'

'Better she than me,' Brenda say, laughing as if is a big joke.

'Enough of all this bickering,' I say sternly, 'remember I no

127

longer tolerate discord and dissension.'

'Can I keep this proof?' Bobbie ask. 'I want to study the story.'

'Sure,' she say, 'Moses or your betrothed can read it for you.'

'Don't carry your insults to the point of absurdity, Brenda,' I rebuff.

'Don't you know?' she ask with wide eyes. 'Bobbie cannot read or write. He is illiterate, but being as he's white we say he is suffering from dyslexia.'

There was a deadly silence. Then Jeannie cried, 'Oh!' and fled to the kitchen.

I was thunderstruck. 'Is this true, Bobbie?'

'I thought you knew,' he say quietly.

'Like I've always said, Moses,' Brenda smirk, 'your pretence at intelligence never fooled me. Bobbie has been living with you all this time, and you don't know the first thing about him. Why do you think he's always looking at those trashy comic books like a juvenile?'

'How did you find out?' I ask weakly.

'That night be brought me that crap you're writing. I had to read it for him.'

I winced. Bobbie glance at me, as if ill-at-ease about the revival of this unhappy memory, wondering how I would take the re-opening of the old wound.

'Truth will out,' I splutter, clutching at the first homily that come to my head to save my face. 'I'd have found out sooner or later.'

'Sooner for me, later for you,' Brenda crow, and went away, shaking with diabolical laughter.

I tried hard to control my shame. Not shame for Bobbie's illiteracy, but for my own dull-wittedness. I remember now, how, on a Sunday morning when we was reading the papers, Bobbie would go through them quickly, refraining from comment, waiting for me to take the lead in discussing the news. And that time when Jeannie wrote, how I read the letter for him. And other times, becoming significant now in retrospective. Galahad was right. Brenda was right. Faizull was right. Paki was right. Even F-and-C, and BP, if they did come to know me better, would of all agree that I was a wet cunt of the first water.

I dried that image with some difficulty, and turned my

128

thoughts to this poor white man who could not read nor write. I could understand the ignorance of black, backwards people, but I have a soft spot for whites. It was beyond my ken that Bobbie didn't know that c-a-t make cat. I was sure that it was Brenda's idea of a hideous joke.

'A-for-apple?' I say coaxingly.

Bobbie look at me blankly.

'B-for-bat?' I try again.

'What's up with you?' he ask.

'Don't look so bloody pleased with yourself,' I say, 'you don't have to bask in your darkness.'

'I get by okay,' he shrug.

'I'll have to send you to one of them ESN schools,' I say thoughtfully, 'with all them little piccaninnies and Pakis. You should of told me when I first interviewed you to be my aide. Now so, you would have passed your First Primer at least.'

'Oh come off it, Moses. It doesn't bother me. Why should you worry?'

'You'll have to excuse me,' I say sarcastically, 'it is the first time that I have come across a fully-fledged white man in this day and age who does not know that A is for apple and B is for bat.'

'Fiddlesticks. What difference does it make? I've managed to conduct my own business, and yours.'

'That is probably why we are up shit-creek,' I say. 'It is not only shattering news. It is nerve-racking. For one thing, how are you going to sign the Registry when you marry Jeannie? Have you thought about that?'

'Of course. I have cleared that up with the Registrar. Look, Moses, you're not going to let a little thing like that come between us?'

'Your ignorance reflects on me,' I say gloomily. 'It's no wonder I am a laughing-stock.'

'Brenda is a bitch. She promised to keep mum.'

'Never mind,' I say kindly. 'I won't tell a soul. But surely it can't be as bad as all that! Come,' I say, getting the little telephone book what we had, with a tiny pencil strap alongside, for writing messages. 'Watch carefully.' I make letter A. 'That's A-for-apple. You must of seen it when you reading all them comic books.'

'Are you being sarky with me?' Bobbie say.

'Try to make A, Bobbie,' I urge. 'It is the first letter of the alphabet. If you learn one, you will soon learn the whole alphabet down to Z. Then we will proceed to simple words and sentences, like Dan-is-the-man-in-the-van.'

But instead of taking my sympathetic concern in the spirit in which it was meant, Bobbie begin to get vex.

'Enough of this child's play, Moses,' he say, 'you are starting to annoy me.'

'Okay,' I sigh, giving up reluctantly. 'But remember it is never too late to learn. You are going to be a married man shortly. Think what pleasure it will give Jeannie when you write your first letter.'

'I'll leave all the writing to you,' he jeered, getting back at me, 'at least I do not hang my hat beyong my reach.'

Jeannie come back from the kitchen bringing cans of cold beer.

'Has that abominable creature gone?' she ask.

'Yes,' I say. 'You must not allow Brenda to upset you. She has her good points.'

'I hope you're not inviting her to our wedding,' she tell Bobbie.

'Talking about that,' I say, glad to get away from the brain-blowing shock of Bobbie's illiteracy, 'what are your plans?'

'We're not having anything big,' Bobbie say.

'You're inviting Jeannie's folk, though? And your own relatives?'

'No Moses,' Jeannie say. 'We want a quiet wedding. We're not having any reception. And we've decided to postpone the honeymoon.'

'Well,' I say, 'to each his own. I do not know the correct procedures when it comes to that.'

Suffice it to say, then, that it was a white wedding; that Galahad come in BP's Mercedes and drive me and Brenda and the prospective bride and groom to the Registry office; ('Listen Brenda,' I say, 'keep your claws out of Jeannie today. It is the happiest day of her life, and you are only present because we could not rustle up another witness'); that Bobbie had been practising and was able to record his name in the Registry; that I take advantage of my perogative as best man to give Jeannie a French kiss; that on the way back we meet up in a accident with a bus 88 and had was to leave Galahad behind literally weeping at the big dent in the front left-hand fender of the Mercedes and make the rest of our way afoot; that Brenda went straight down to the basement when we reach home; that Brenda give them a year's free subscription to the paper as a present, and I give them an electric steam iron, and Galahad forgot to bring his present and promise to pass around some time and drop it.

The three of we what remain make a toast with sherry.

'To you and Jeannie,' I say to Bobbie. 'I deeply regret that it is not a more celebrative gathering, but this is the way you wanted it. However, may all your Christmases be white.'

'Hear hear,' Bobbie say.

'You have been so good to us, Moses,' Jeannie say.

'I have done nothing,' I say modestly.

After a few sherries Bobbie advance to whisky and begin to feel thirsty.

'Let's go down to our room,' he tell Jeannie.

'We can't leave poor Moses all alone,' Jeannie protest.

'In any case,' I clear my throat, 'you are not leaving me. I am leaving you.'

'What do you mean?' she cry.

'I mean I am giving you the penthouse as a honeymoon suite for the night,' I say magnaminously. 'I will sleep in your room.'

'Are you sure, old boy?' Bobbie say, ever anxious for my welfare. 'Will you be comfortable enough?'

'This is too much,' Jeannie say.

'Too much is not enough for you, Jeannie,' I say.

'Oh Moses,' she say.

▲ ▲ ▲ ▲

Thus I maintained my resolve to do good unto others, and bring a little sunshine into the lives of those less fortunate than I.

As the days went by it look like we was in for a halcyon spell. Bobbie and Jeannie shared the domestic chores, and if he was busy he send Jeannie up to attend to my needs. The three of us live in perfect harmony, watching the television together,

131

sharing our meals, and she and me had great fun teaching Bobbie the alphabet, though he still look at his comic books avidly.

The only fly in the ointment was that Jeannie was discontent with the accommodation they had. Not that she complained to me, but Bobbie said how she was wishing they had a flat like mines, so she could feel they was living in a real home instead of one room.

'You know you're welcome to come up any time you like,' I remind him.

'I know that,' he sigh, 'but it isn't the same as if it were ours. Poor Jeannie. Sometimes I think she is too good for me, and that you are right about my being uneducated.'

'Take courage,' I say. 'You are making excellent progress. You are down to V now, and Z is just around the corner. When you get there we might try one of those rapid English courses.'

'You know Moses,' he say, 'you are one in a million. Were it not for your friendship, I don't know what would have become of me. Have you heard any news from Galahad?'

'I think the Party is waiting for a delegation of Black Panthers from the States, headed by BP. It appears that he went back for reinforcements, and is returning to make some drastic changes in the administration of the Establishment. Heads will roll, they say, and BP wants to convert Enoch Powell and make him President of the Black Power movement in Brit'n. The trial palls by comparison with such a gigantic undertaking.'

'I'm glad they'll have that on their minds,' Bobbie say. Jeannie was afraid I might be called upon to give evidence. Not for any racial reasons, but she just wants to live a quiet happy life, like we do here.'

'Amen to that,' I say, 'see how I have divorced myself from squabble and fray, and am all the better for it.'

Indeed, I had never had it so good. Jeannie's presence was like having a young fairy godmother in the house. Not only was she a good and conscientious char, but she was such a charming girl, ready to bestow favours, and even used to go down to the basement and chat with Brenda to show that she had no ill feelings.

In return for her generous nature, I was ever willing to offer

132

my services, no matter how menial the task. One of these was the scrubbing of her back whenever she had a bath. Like most people she found it difficult to get at that part of her anatomy, even with a brush, and it gave me great pleasure to assist her whenever Bobbie was not available; it seemed such a little thing for the countless jobs she did.

I was preoccupied with this one day when Bobbie come in unexpectedly.

'Hello hello,' he say, 'what's all this then?'

Shit couldn't fly off a shovel as fast as I thought in that moment, dear R.

'You're in the nick of time,' I say, 'I have just come. To a momentous decision.'

'Fine words won't save you Moses,' he say, brandishing his fist aloft like he seen the Power boys do. 'This is the end.'

'Wait until you hear what I have to say,' I entreated.

'I'll give you five seconds,' he say, looking at his watch.

'The penthouse is yours,' I say.

'Fine words,' he begin, then stop. 'Come again?' he query.

I suppose I could be facetious and say that I said joyfully, 'If you insist,' but it wasn't like that at all. I do not know if you have ever been caught with your trousers down, in *flagrento delicto* or whatever it is lords and ladies call it, but I can tell you that I was *trimbling* with shock and fear. What I blathered was, 'The-penthouse-is-yours' again, and continue, as I see him consider this, 'Doesn't that put a different complexion on things?'

'You have behaved like a despicable cad,' Bobbie say. 'You realize your paltry offer can never make amends for your loathsome behaviour?'

I nodded silently, hanging my head.

'If I do decide to accept, it will have to be on my own terms,' he say.

'You're the boss,' I say.

'How could you, how could you?' he burst out now.

'It was a weak moment,' I say. 'To err is human,'

'Things can never be the same with us,' he say sadly. 'You had better go and pack your things.'

▲ ▲ ▲ ▲

Thus are the mighty fallen, empires totter, monarchs de-throne
and the walls of Pompeii bite the dust. Humiliated and degraded,
I took up abode in Bobbie's erstwhile room, while he and
Jeannie move in to the penthouse. Bobbie did set down some
ironclad conditions and would not budge or display the slightest
inclination for compromise or compassion, but instead fortified
his position by stipulating penalties for defaulting.

'Can't I even come up to look at Upstairs and Downstairs in
colour?' I plead. 'We used to enjoy that programme so much
together.'

'You've got a television in the room,' he say.

'It won't be the same, Bobbie.'

He made a harsh laugh. 'Nothing will ever be the same. And
for one thing, "Bobbie" is for my friends. You'd better begin to
call me Robert.'

'All right,' I say, summoning a little dignity. 'I won't belittle
myself any further. It's a great price you ask for a slight
indiscretion, though.'

I suppose I should be grateful that he did not confiscate my
Memoirs. Perhaps he felt that would be the unkindest cut of all,
and some grudging modicum of pity must have moved him to
concede it.

But it was small consolation, cooped up in that small
enclosure. The first night I wake up screaming from claustropho-
bia. Small consolation, too, that Messrs Robert and Jeannie were
paying rent for the penthouse – it was one of his cunning moves to
secure tenancy, for these days, with them new rent laws, you
have to wonder who is the potter, pray, and who the pot. I was
reduced to living as a tenant in my own house, with Robert
holding the reins and cracking the whip.

You might wonder what Ashby-de-la-Zouch had to say for
herself while I was doing penance. She was not without sympathy
and understanding. Indeed, she saw no reason why I could not
continue to scrub her back as opportunity knocked, but I was
incapacitated by the stringent punishment for any infringements
of the Master's regulations. It was lusting for white pussy that
brought bad blood 'tween Robert and I, and all I could hope for

134

was that the tables would turn and I would be returned to my rightful position as head of the house. Perhaps I may be allowed one comment here, how it is a pity that Adam had that spare rib what God make Eve with, for from the moment woman came into this world it was as if a Pandora Box open and let loose evils in Paradise. All this talk about woman's lib, left to me, I would chain the whole lot of them to the railings in Downing Street, and left them there to attract foreign currency from the tourists.

Things was so bad that even the unsavoury Paki was taking a turn in my arse, presuming on my company whenever he like, without even knocking on the door.

'How long are you going to be slumming?' he ask, pushing aside my papers and hoisting a leg up on the table. He even blow cigarette smoke in my face.

'Don't be silly,' I say, 'can't you see I am getting more rent by letting out the penthouse and living here?'

'You really had it cushy up there, though,' he say.

'This is just a temporary measure,' I say. 'Sometimes you have to tighten your belt.'

'You look as if you're strangling, though.'

I suppose I must of seemed a little gaunt and hollow-eyed.

'I haven't been sleeping well,' I say.

'You ought to do some Yoga,' he say. 'Look at me, fit as a fiddle. Try this for sleeplessness.' And he went in the corner and stand on his head, and cross his legs and make an X.

'That's cool,' I say. 'Does it work?'

'Try it,' he urge, upsided down, 'your worries will disappear and you'll feel a new man.'

'Okay,' I say, to get rid of him, 'I'll give it a whirl when I have the odd moment.'

He come upright. 'There are some other postures, for different complaints,' he say, hawking Yoga like a salesman. 'For instance, if you are depressed, try this.' He wrap himself in a knot, hands and feet going every which way. 'You see?'

'Yeah,' I say, 'I'll try that one after I become proficient.'

'Just help me to get up,' he say struggling, 'I seem to be in a bit of a tangle.'

But I leave the bastard right there until he unravel himself and went away.

Paki's visits were innocent, but I can't say the same for Brenda when she heard I had shifted. There were no flies on her.

'There's more in the mortar than the pestle, Moses,' she say, hitting on the truth right away. 'Bob must of caught you with Jeannie. I knew there would be trouble when that bitch came.'

'Ha,' I make a half-laugh. 'Even were it so, why should I come here? I tell you it's an economic necessity. They're paying rent, you know.'

'More fool you,' she say, 'you'll never get them out now. However, I'm glad in a way that you are making changes. I want to extend the basement.'

'Pardon?' I say.

'Party business is getting brisk and back on its feet now that BP is coming back. The pressure of work is so great, that I have had to encroach on my living quarters. You ought to see the small room I live in behind the office. It's so crowded I might as well move into the Pakis' abbatoir in the back garden.'

'Why don't you just clear out and shift the whole caboodle from my house?' I snarl.

'Don't be facetious,' she say coldly. 'We're entrenched here. For keeps.'

'Maybe I could sell the house to the Party and clear out myself,' I say seriously.

'You'll be lucky to sell this white elephant,' she smirk.

'Well, I don't give two fucks about your problems,' I say. 'I've got enough of my own.'

'You could try to get that Aussie out, cut off his water and gas or something.'

'I'm not that sort of landlord,' I say.

'No?' she sneer. 'You'll plumb the lowest depths if needs be. Don't think I have been blind to the going-ons in this house.'

'What do you mean?' I say, taking umbrage. 'You have the effrontery to stand there and suggest all is not above board? The only disrespectability in this house is in the basement.'

'Bah,' she say. 'I got enough on you to cook your goose.'

I laugh uneasily. 'Would you like a drink?' I say. 'I've only got sherry, 'twas all I was able to bring down with me, what remain after the toasting when Robert get married.'

'Fetch it, then.'

136

I started to call my footman, and had to laugh ruefully, and get up and fetch it myself.

After a few sherries, she begin to be flattering an complimentary. 'You know, Moses,' she say, 'I might have been a bit premature in assessing your memoirs.'

'Hump,' I say, waiting breathless for her next word.

'There are possibilities,' she say. 'Of course, it will never see the light of day through any reputable English publisher, but I may be able to edit and use extracts in our paper.'

I stiffened. 'I haven't written for the hoi-polloi,' I say loftily. 'It does not matter if I get a limited edition, as I know it will only appeal to highbrows and eggheads.'

'This is the only chance you'll get,' she say.

'No thank you,' I say, 'I would rather die that cast pearls before swine.'

'You refuse my offer?'

'Point-blank,' I say unhesitatingly.

'Then,' she say, 'instead of cajolement, I will have to employ threat. You have driven me to it.'

'You've got nothing on me,' I say uneasily.

'What about the trafficking of illegal Paki immigrants,' she say, showing her true colours.

'That's a thing of the past,' I wave it aside.

'You can get two or three years for a thing like that if I testify to your criminality.'

I laugh hollowly. 'You must be joking.'

'There are other things,' she hinted darkly, 'such as, for instance, cuckolding with dear Jeannie? Imagine your status if such knowledge came to the attention of the public!'

'Have another sherry,' I say, procrastinating desperately. 'I don't know what you're getting at.'

'I will come to the point,' she say. 'You will vacate this room to me. It's possible for a man to live in the basement, but a woman has her pride. It will suit you admirably. Having rose from zero you have little needs. You've only been indulging yourself with all these luxuries.'

'You can't be serious!' I ejaculate.

'You'll also be able to keep an eye on things for me,' she say. 'There are some genteel whites who pass and fling literal shit through the window. I haven't been successful in catching any of them myself.'

I make a strangling sound, commingling it with other torturous cries.

'Reduced to cleaning up white shit!' I gasp. 'You can't prove a thing, Brenda.'

'Couldn't I?' she mock. 'Between me and Paki we'll send you down the river for a long stretch.'

'Aha!' I cry, 'now I know you're bluffing – you don't have any truck with him.'

For answer she went in the corner and do the very same handstand that Paki did, irregardless of her skirt falling down like a parachute and exposing the shadowy V of her treasury.

▲ ▲ ▲ ▲

Little more remains to be said. Galahad offer to swap his basement room for mine, as he wanted to be stationed at headquarters, but I wanted, like a stout-hearted British captain, to go down with the sinking ship.

'Ah Moses,' he say contritely, 'what a let-down you have suffered.'

'What can I tell you?' I say, kicking aside a batch of Lamming's *Water For Berries* that was in my way to stand up by the window. I looked out over the back garden, remembering Faizull and the slaughter of the lamb. Them was good days, comparatively speaking. 'There is no god but Mohammed,' I mutter.

'What?' Galahad ask.

'Nothing,' I say. 'What news from the bridge?'

'He's doing the Rapid English Course now,' he say. 'I am helping him with pronunciations, you know what an awful accent these Northerners have.'

'And Jeannie?'

'A bit of a problem, Moses,' Galahad confide. 'She always wants to have a bath when I'm there, and insists I should scrub her back if he isn't around. What can I do but comply?'

I surveyed the miniature jungle I could see out of the window, wondering if I should start from scratch all over again, forage amongst the undergrowth and grub for acorns and truffles.

Only once, up to the time of writing did Robert deign to visit me. I opened my heart. 'Well come and welcome,' I say, hoping the greeting might stir a wisp of fond memory.

'Cut that shit out,' he say, stumbling over a stack of *Power*, the new paper, and a big crate of Baldwin's *The Fire Next Time*. 'I'm only here because I've got a small query you might be able to clear up.'

'Glad to be of service, Robert,' I say humbly. 'Speak your piece and depart before you become contaminated.'

'It's about the conjugation of verbs,' he say. 'How can you tell which is transitive when the pluperfect is irregular, and the past participle is superlative?'

'You stump me there, Robert,' I admit. 'Verbs was never my forte, paricularly the irregular ones. But my! You've certainly made great strides!'

'Haven't I?' He couldn't help a bit of strutting. 'I bet I can write better memoirs than you!'

I didn't make a direct reply to that one, I merely shrug and say, '*Quien sabe?*'

'I'm doing French too,' he say, 'but I haven't come across that one. What with our entry into the Common Market, it will stand me in good stead.'

'I cannot tell you how pleased I am,' I say. 'You will go far, Robert, like children's shoes.'

'Yeah. Well,' he look around the storeroom, books and papers and a pighead I did salvage from a demonstration to make a little souse, and a pair of Brenda's dirty panties hook up on a chair from an interlude the night before. 'How goes it with you?'

'Things are black, as you can see,' I say, 'but every dog has his day. I'm sorry I've nothing to offer you, unless you'd like a cup of tea and what's left of the toad-in-a-hole I had for supper?'

'No. I've eaten. It's all right. Well, I guess that's it, then.'

'Yeah,' I say, 'that's it.'

'Good luck.'

'You too.'

One final word. It occurs to me that some black power militants might chose to misconstrue my Memoirs for their own purposes, and put the following moral to defame me, to wit: that after the ballad and the episode, it is the white man who ends up

Upstairs and the black man who ends up Downstairs.

But I have an epilogue up my sleeve. For old time's sake Robert still knocks one with Brenda on and off. What I plot to do is to go up top, and not only inform Jeannie of his infidelity, but arrange for the both of we to catch Master Robert in *flagrento delicto*, when I will fling down the gauntlet.